CAROL CANNON
MA, CADC

Hooked *on*
Unhappiness

Breaking the cycle
of discontent

Blessings to you!
Carol Cannon

Pacific Press® Publishing Association
Nampa, Idaho
Oshawa, Ontario, Canada
www.pacificpress.com

Cover design by Michelle C. Petz
Cover design resources from iStockphoto.com/Ressy
Inside design by Steve Lanto

Additional copies of this book are available by calling toll-free
1-800-765-6955 or online at www.adventistbookcenter.com.

ISBN 13: 978-0-8163-2260-2
ISBN 10: 0-8163-2260-0

08 09 10 11 12 • 5 4 3 2 1

Dedication

This book is lovingly and hopefully dedicated to the next generation of recovering people: my sons, Paul and Kurt, and grandchildren—Austin, Cody, Katie, Levi, and Lila.

Also by Carol Cannon

Never Good Enough: Growing Up Imperfect in a "Perfect" Family

Contents

Introduction

The minute Pam wakes up in the morning, she catalogs her aches and pains so she will be ready to offer a detailed description to the first person she meets. At breakfast, she responds to her teenage son's friendly "Whazzup?" with a groan. She didn't sleep well. She's exhausted, and the pain in her shoulder is worse. While eating her Cheerios, Pam obsesses about her to-do list. An unresolved problem assails her and attaches itself to the amorphous mass already rolling around in her head. Her face takes on a worried expression. As if on cue, her husband asks what's wrong. She launches into a litany of her woes. When she looks up, he has disappeared.

Do you know any good, kind, moral people who seem to suffer the tortures of the damned? They take pride in being poor in spirit. They seem to relish being persecuted for righteousness' sake. The Bible says there's a time for everything—happiness, joy, pain, and sorrow. But for these unhappy souls, the cloud of gloom never lifts. They can't escape the slough of despond, no matter how hard they try. They can't *not* be miserable.

Some try to dispel their negative feelings by analyzing them. Others attempt to counteract their pessimism with positive affirmations. Those who think God requires His followers to be hap, hap, happy all the time memorize Scripture or pray unceasingly to ward off the demons of discouragement. If that doesn't work, they feel guilty and get even more depressed.

If you or anyone you love fits this description, I have good news—intractable misery is not a failure of faith. Nor is it a sign of weakness or perversity. And it definitely is not your fault. If you suffer (and I do mean *suffer*) from chronic misery and unhappiness, there's hope. Negaholism is treatable. If you've spent your whole life struggling with gloom, doom, and despair, you've got nothing to lose and a lot to gain by reading on.

Ask yourself the following questions to see if you are a certifiable negaholic: Do you find yourself in a bad mood more often than not? Are you critical of everyone and everything around you? Do you dwell on painful memories? Do you have a negative perspective of global proportions? When someone says, "Good morning," do you think, *What's good about it?* [1]

If complaining is your favorite pastime, if you have turned venting and lamenting into an art form, this book is for you. It is possible to break the chronic misery habit.

I couldn't help noticing, while I was growing up in the shadow of numerous religious institutions, that churches are often hotbeds of misery addiction and undue self-sacrifice (martyring). Frankly, I don't believe churches have an exclusive claim on the misery and martyr syndrome. Misery addiction is a disease—a miasma of unhealthy attitudes, beliefs, and behaviors that has infiltrated our whole society from the beauty salon to the boardroom, from the supermarket to the sports arena. We all love to criticize, complain, and anticipate disaster. God save us from our self-pity!

Note to religious-oriented readers: while I consider myself to be a conservative Christian, I have chosen not to make this book an occasion for moralizing or a pulpit from which to preach my personal religious convictions. Along with my religious beliefs, I am gratefully steeped in the traditions of twelve-step programs, which are deeply spiritual but which suggest that "we have no opinion on outside issues." Religion may be a part of spirituality, but it is not synonymous with it.

A word of thanks to my peers in recovery, my sponsor, and my colleagues—past and present—at The Bridge to Recovery. Special gratitude to Nancy Green, my personal assistant, and to Paul, my eternally optimistic partner.

---

1. Sheri and Bob Stritof, "Is Negativity Hurting Your Marriage?" About.com: Marriage, http://marriage.about.com/cs/communicationkeys/a/negativity.htm.

Chapter 1

Confessions of a Workaholic Worrywart

I guess I just prefer to see the dark side of things. The glass is always half empty.
And cracked. And I just cut my lip on it. And chipped a tooth.

— Janeane Garofalo

Some time ago, an omnicheerful friend informed me that I was the most pessimistic person she had ever met. Excuse me? You mean it's not normal to look at life through grim-tinted glasses? I thought I was just being realistic! My family and friends (a bunch of cockeyed optimists) were aware of my negativism. The mailman and newspaper carrier probably noticed it too, but *I* didn't see how negatively oriented I was, nor did I consider my attitude to be unhealthy. I was the last person in my world to recognize that I was hooked on unhappiness.

My attention and energy were drawn to crises and chaos, tragedy and trauma, as surely as a moth is drawn to the flame. I couldn't imagine how everyone around me could be so oblivious to the harsh realities of life. The sky was falling, the earth was crumbling beneath us, and waves were rolling over us. Why wasn't anyone else concerned?

Whoever was in charge around there obviously needed a personal assistant, but I didn't see anyone standing in line to apply for the job. Well, *I* was willing to oblige. (How's *that* for grandiosity?) I appointed myself adjutant to the Almighty and set about trying to rescue and repair everyone and everything I considered problematic. While trying to arrange the universe to *my* satisfaction, thinking it was synonymous with *God's,* I overlooked the obvious: *I* was the one who was out of control. *I* was the one who was crazy—as in "Local Nutcase Tries to Save the World"!

Hooked on unhappiness

In my compulsive efforts to manage the universe, *my* life became unmanageable. I worried incessantly about all the pain and suffering around me. Worrying gave me an illusion of control. It allowed me to manage people and circumstances within the confines of my mind.

My constant obsessing created enormous anxiety, which demanded more worrying, which generated even greater anxiety. If I wasn't alarmed or upset about something, I thought I was out of touch with reality! I was like a nervous puppy chasing her tail. Worrying became an endless loop. I tied myself in proverbial knots.

Mulling over worst-case scenarios put me in fight-or-flight mode, stimulating an adrenaline rush. I might as well have been getting high on amphetamines. When the flood of adrenaline drained away, I was left exhausted and depressed like Elijah after his enervating experience on Mount Carmel.[1]

Eventually, my endocrine system got stuck in high gear. I couldn't "let go and let God." Convinced that He needed my help, I worked twenty-four hours a day, seven days a week.[2] The crash that followed my worry-and-work binges was like the withdrawal syndrome drug addicts go through when the high wears off. I was in a state of adrenaline depletion. To get rid of the unpleasant hangover, I simply shifted into hyperdrive and launched into another project. Full speed ahead!

In order to maintain a consistent supply of adrenaline, I added caretaking to my repertoire. Rescuing people allowed me to work harder, worry longer, and manage better. It was a toxic combination. I progressed from (1) seeing the bleak side of every situation, to (2) worrying about the disastrous consequences of failing to fix everything that was broken and quite a few things that *weren't* broken, to (3) begging God for miracles, to (4) working myself half to death trying to answer my own prayers. This cycle gave me a sense of purpose. Perhaps I took the Busy Bee program in Pathfinder Club a little too seriously.

Eye-popping anxiety haunted my every waking moment and most of my sleeping moments too. When I succeeded in conquering a given challenge, thus momentarily removing the *cause* of my worries, I found temporary relief. Seconds later, another crisis would come along, and I would go crazy trying to fix *it* or rescue *them*.

Can you identify with this description? I like to think I'm not alone in my insanity. Focusing on other people's problems helped me avoid my own fears. The changes in brain chemistry that took place when I was in the groove were autointoxicating. Who needs a dealer? I manufactured my own stimulants, thank you very much.

There's every probability that I had a neurological problem that I was unaware of—a biochemical deficit for which I was unconsciously compensating. John Ratey, clinical professor of psychiatry at Harvard Medical School, believes that addictive behavior is associated with a faulty novelty and reward system that he has dubbed the *reward deficiency syndrome.*[3] Apparently, I had that problem before it had a name! When drug abusers tax their systems with alcohol, marijuana, cocaine, and heroin, they are messing up the communications between the neurons in their brains. When I taxed my system with stimulating activities and processes, I was messing up the communications between the neurons in my brain in a similar fashion. Me—a drug addict! Who knew?

Childhood days

Did I become an adrenaline junkie all by myself? Was it my idea to turn my life into a sacrificial statement? Did I invent my addiction to misery? Actually, I think my paternal grandfather provided the dominant gene. Grandpa has an alarmist personality which contributed to my being physiologically and psychologically vulnerable from birth or before. According to author John Powell, "the process of osmosis by which children absorb their parents' vision of reality actually begins with intrauterine or prenatal influences."[4] Apparently, a misery addict's predisposition to negativity is born before she or he is!

My mother, a red-white-and-blue-blooded American girl, was pregnant with me when Pearl Harbor was attacked in 1941. That event must have jarred her the way 9/11 shocked us. The hyper-amygdaloid storms in her brain affected my fetal environment. (The arousal of the amygdala

is related to feelings of stress and anxiety.) Mom's elevated stress hor-
mones coursed through my body, which may have set me up to be an
anxious child. If so, I wasn't alone.

One wonders how many children born today are affected biochemi-
cally by terrorism, tsunamis, and other tragedies. There's no doubt in my
mind that I was hardwired to be a nervous, anxious, negative person. An
article in the *New York Times* (November 1996) validated this. Citing a
study reported in the prestigious journal *Science,* it linked a specific gene
to people who are neurologically more vulnerable to stressful life events
than others.[5]

Sensitive to the physical and emotional threats in my universe, I tod-
dled around in a state of irrepressible uneasiness. It was like growing up
in the war zone of an alcoholic family—a place where children live in
constant fear of what may happen next.

The 1950s were not "happy days" for me. While in elementary school, I
was exposed to daily news broadcasts about the Korean conflict. Fascinated
with Bible prophecy, my grandfather insisted that the undeclared nonwar
was a fulfillment of scriptural warnings regarding wars and rumors of wars,
which meant that the second advent of Christ was imminent. We had to
prepare for the coming of the Lord, lest we be destroyed in the lake of fire
that was going to consume the wicked when Jesus came. So you'd better be
good, little girl. If God doesn't get you, Santa Claus will.

Grandpa's fire-and-brimstone preaching scared me as much as the
war did. Many children reared in religious homes are exposed to similar
beliefs. I may have been more sensitive than the average kid—I don't
know. I just know that I lived in a state of unrelenting terror. Today, my
heart goes out to children who are exposed prematurely to church doctrines that generate overwhelming fear. Recently I asked my husband, a
pastoral counselor, at what age he thought children should be taught
end-time theology. "When they're about twenty-five," he replied.

As an adolescent, I wouldn't even have *considered* using our national
sedative, alcohol, to relieve my fears. I had been told that drinking was a
sin punishable by death. If you drink, you do not pass *GO,* you do not
collect $200, you go straight to the lake of fire or hell or purgatory or are
left standing alone in a field while everyone else is raptured (depending
on which prophetic interpretation your church of choice embraces).

I had to find a way to anesthetize my feelings—one that God would not frown upon. So I set out to find a way to improve my emotional ecology without incurring His or Dad's wrath. In terms of psychologist Lawrence Kohlberg's classic stages of moral development, I was right on schedule.[6] Preadolescent that I was, I wasn't morally mature enough to seek God. I was interested only in avoiding the lake of fire and the tribulation that preceded it.

Perhaps if I tried to be perfect, if I could figure out how to earn both Dad's and God's approval, I would stand a better chance of making it out alive. Aha! Maybe I could become so indispensable to God that He would *have* to spare me. This survival scheme was not a random choice. It was, in fact, very creative. Both heredity and environment dictated my decision.

Not only was I terrified of the future—the present was pretty daunting too. My dad was financially stressed, and my mom was clinically depressed. On a mood scale of 1 to 10, Mom registered somewhere between -2 and +1. Her emotional state became my reference point for normal. She modeled negativity to me, and I was genetically predisposed to it as well.

I distinctly remember feeling maligned and misunderstood by the age of ten. By the time I hit junior high school, I had adopted a persistently pessimistic outlook on life. I was not the bundle of optimism, enthusiasm, and energy that teenagers are meant to be.

Trying to win approval

Because I thought it was my duty to make Mom and Dad happy, I began to overachieve, overwork, and overdo everything. I evolved, rather ungraciously, into a full-blown workaholic and a world-class "worksaholic" (legalist), straining myself to gain the approval and acceptance of both God and man. *I was driven to justify my existence in the here and now and to earn my eternal salvation as well.* Does that sound like a normal adolescent to you?

I recall the first time I received a compliment for doing a kind deed. My freshman year in high school, I gave a couple of items from my own meager wardrobe to a needy classmate. As far as I know, my motive was unselfish, but when I was commended publicly for my kind act, I was instantly hooked on adulation. Here was the affirmation I had been looking for all my life. The needy little puppy dog started to wag her tail.

From then on, I was willing to do almost anything to earn accolades. I systematically sacrificed myself to win approval, carrying altruism to such an extreme that I nearly destroyed myself, figuratively, if not literally. I *may* have come close to killing my "caregivees" with kindness too. Being helpful boosted my ego. It shored up my sagging self-esteem. I deluded myself into thinking that I was just unselfish by nature.

If I could have seen myself as others saw me, I might have questioned my motives. I sighed frequently and loudly and complained to anyone who would listen. Gradually, I perfected my "poor me" persona. Moaning and groaning, whining and complaining are the martyr's way of leaking anger out obliquely and siphoning attention from unsuspecting sympathizers. I considered myself a victim, but I wasn't. I was a *volunteer*!

In *Codependents' Guide to the Twelve Steps,* Melody Beattie describes how negativism affected her intimate relationships: "I had little to offer friends, except my perpetual complaints about the misery of my life. Most of my friendships centered around shared stories of victimization. [I call this *bonding by martyring*.]

"I had no feelings that I was aware of . . . no needs that I was aware of. I prided myself in my ability to endure needless suffering, deprive myself, and go without."[7]

Beattie's modus operandi was mine too. I caught myself thinking that God had singled me out to carry a heavier-than-average burden because He knew I could handle it. When I finally woke up and smelled my superior attitude, I was mortified.

Workaholism, caretaking, and control became a self-perpetuating cycle. By the age of forty-five, I was toast—burned out from overwork and overworry. I knew I had to change. I tried to tear myself away from my obsessive-compulsive behavior. But I couldn't. At first, I didn't realize what that indicated. I was a certified alcohol and drug counselor by then, *and I didn't recognize my own behavior as addictive.* Talk about delusion and denial!

Admitting defeat

The truth was that I had a martyr monkey on my back. Actually, it was a giant gorilla—King Kong with a shave, as one charismatic preacher used to say. Wake up and smell the Postum, little Miss! You are spiritually bankrupt and seriously in need of treatment services yourself!

That was twenty years ago. I'd like to report that I called a therapist immediately and made an appointment, but I didn't. I wasn't *that* healthy. Instead, I spent several months in a futile effort to fix myself. After all, I'm a treatment professional. I *should* be able to cure myself. Wrong! An avid churchgoer, I also presumed that if I had enough faith, God would heal me instantly. I didn't want to waste my time and *His* money on therapy (a little manipulation there), so I prayed harder instead.

Meanwhile, because I was oriented to salvation by works, I read every self-help book on the market. Alas, I couldn't put their suggestions into practice. Terry Kellogg, author and counselor, says that knowledge only makes an addict a more informed prisoner. No kidding! I couldn't translate good ideas into new behavior because I had not yet experienced adequate pain or a sense of personal powerlessness. I hadn't run out of track. I hadn't yet experienced enough discomfort to render me humble, teachable. My home study recovery plan was a complete bust.

The more I tried to control my behavior, the more I lost control. *Puff, puff. Chug, chug.* I was the little engine that couldn't. Months later, finally defeated, I admitted myself to a hospital-based treatment program for addiction and codependence—the broad diagnostic category within which compulsive caretaking, control, martyring, and other "clean" addictions fall. My best thinking, believing, and behaving got me there.

A workaholic worrywart, compulsive caretaker, and magnanimous martyr, I had no idea how to arrest the addictions I had denied for so long. I had to admit defeat. I didn't realize it then, but this was my first step toward recovery.

Negaholism undermined my character, sabotaged valued relationships, and subverted my spirituality, just as alcoholism does. The damage that clean addictions inflicted on my body and soul was identical to the damage that chemical dependence inflicts on alcoholics and drug addicts. I ended up in a treatment center full of alcoholics, because, like them, I was suffering from a deadly illness. My problem was bigger than I was, bigger than all the resources I could muster from within myself. I had a primary, chronic, progressive, fatal illness that I couldn't cure on my own. I could not arrest my out-of-control behavior, and I could not manage the consequences.

Recovery is a process

Where my attempts to gain knowledge and insight failed to fix me, the spiritual program of Alcoholics Anonymous succeeded. While I was in treatment, I was required to attend AA meetings. There, I discovered that the same program that works for alcoholics works for negaholics too—and for food addicts and relationship junkies and control freaks, etc.

Because all addictions are basically suicide on the installment plan, I now consider misery addiction to be the granddaddy of all addictions. Obviously I'm not using the term *addiction* in the strictest technical sense here. Martyring, misery, caretaking, control, and many other codependent behaviors are deeply ingrained habits that may or may not be considered addictive disorders per se. They certainly aren't described as such in the lexicon of mental health professionals! But where recovery is concerned, they respond rather well to twelve-step programs. For that reason, I think of most excessive behaviors as addictions and address them as addictions in my personal and professional life.

Longstanding, deep-seated habits don't go away overnight. You can't simply dismiss them or casually wave them off. Recovery is a process, not an event. I began to change when I accepted the fact that I could not conquer my problems single-handedly.

Little by little, I woke up to the realization that it was OK to admit defeat. It was actually a relief. I could stop trying to accomplish the impossible. It wasn't working anyway! I discovered that *powerlessness* is not synonymous with *helplessness*. To admit my powerlessness was simply to acknowledge my need of help. Welcome to the real world, Carol!

Today, I celebrate the remission of my addiction to misery, one day at a time. I'm not cured, but I no longer enjoy martyring, obsessing, worrying, or being depressed. I don't get high on being mistreated and maligned. I don't set myself up to be abandoned. I prefer peace and serenity to the insanity of overwork, compulsive caretaking, and relentless self-pity. I cherish myself and treat myself with respect. I no longer feel compelled to borrow trouble or beg for burdens.

In *Fully Human, Fully Alive,* author John Powell describes people whose whole lives are like a perennial funeral procession.[8] That was the story of my life. I didn't feel normal unless I was being neglected or rejected. I got high on being "weary, faint, and sore"—a phrase from one of my workaholic grandfather's favorite gospel songs. No more! Do I ever relapse? Yes, but I haven't beat myself up for it lately!

While recovery has its ups and downs, and while the process of growth and change can be challenging, it is easier to pursue health and happiness than to entertain one's misery indefinitely. Letting go of old attitudes and developing new skills takes time, but the end result makes the effort worthwhile. Negaholics *do* recover! Anyone who has a desire to stop being negative *can* abstain from complaining, banish his or her worries, and refuse to whine—one day at a time.

In the ensuing pages, I'll list the characteristics of a martyr, explain what causes negaholism, show how it plays itself out in personal relationships, and describe how to kick the misery habit. Please note that I will be using the terms *addiction to misery, martyring* or *martyrdom, negativism, negaholism, negativity,* and *unhappiness* interchangeably.

Although I consider the negative thinking, believing, behaving habit to be as grave as alcoholism, I want to maintain a positive spirit here. To sob about misery addiction would be to succumb to it. I want to emphasize the light side while recognizing the dark. I'd hate for anyone to get depressed as a result of reading a book about addiction to misery! That's not what I have in mind. So let's laugh at least as much as we cry, dance to a peppy rhythm instead of a mournful tune. We don't even want to come *close* to taking ourselves or our recovery too seriously!

I'd be a real fake if I wrote about addiction to misery without including my own story. It begins with *powerlessness.* Any of the characters in chapter 2 could have been me.

Hope for Today

Most misery addicts think their unhappiness is inextricable, and their friends and family think it's inexcusable! In reality, it's neither. If you are hooked on unhappiness, cut yourself a little slack. It's OK to admit that you have a problem bigger than you and greater than all the resources you can muster from within yourself. Surrendering to your need of help is not the same as succumbing to weakness. Give yourself permission to end the futile struggle with negative thinking. You can't outthink the habit of overthinking. Instead, reach outside yourself for help and support. When you stop trying to do the impossible, you open the door to an array of new possibilities.

Self-Study

1. Which, if any, of the incidents or issues mentioned in this chapter feel familiar to you? Based on your own experience, what do you relate to or identify with the most?
2. Choose one or more feeling words to describe how you are affected by what you have just read (a) happy, (b) hurt, (c) sad, (d) relieved, (e) angry.
3. Are you willing to embrace your truth? If so, write a paragraph describing what you think and feel regarding one or more painful childhood memories.
4. If you feel distressed or overwhelmed after reading this chapter, consider talking with a close friend or therapist about your response. Postpone reading chapter 2 until you have had time to integrate your feelings.

---

1. See 1 Kings 19:4.

2. My theology at that time allowed for only a male God. I no longer think of my Higher Power in terms of gender.

3. John Ratey, *A User's Guide to the Brain: Perception, Attention, and the Four Theaters of the Brain* (New York: Random House, 2001), 118, 123. While brain chemistry unquestionably plays a role in our emotional problems, my emphasis here is on taking responsibility for change. This would include getting an assessment by a viable medical professional to see if medication is indicated.

4. John Powell, *Fully Human, Fully Alive: A New Life Through a New Vision* (Niles, Ill.: Argus Communications, 1976), 63.

5. Edward M. Hallowell, *Worry* (New York: Ballentine Books, 1997), xiv.

6. Lawrence Kohlberg theorized that there are six stages of moral development. In the earlier stages, young children are motivated to engage in socially acceptable behavior by fear of punishment or consequences. They are not mature enough to make ethical decisions based on high-level thought and intention.

7. Melody Beattie, *Codependents' Guide to the Twelve Steps* (New York: Simon & Schuster, 1990), 10.

8. Powell, *Fully Human, Fully Alive,* 21.

CHAPTER 2

Martyrs and Other Assorted Misery Addicts

Voluptuaries, consumed by their senses, always begin by flinging themselves with a great display of frenzy into an abyss. But they survive, they come to the surface again. And they develop a routine of the abyss: "It's four o'clock. At five, I have my abyss."

— Sidonie Gabrielle Collette

Perfect Patsy

Patsy is one of the sweetest women I know. She anticipates other people's needs and fulfills them before they are even aware they *have* a need. She's so good at sensing and satisfying her closest friends' desires that those who benefit from her generosity often accuse her of being clairvoyant. Her friends and family can't imagine how she always notices their wants and wishes before they do.

Patsy enjoys their approval and takes pleasure in being praised. But when her "benefactees" fail to repay her in gratitude, she feels taken advantage of and lapses into self-pity. In her weaker moments, she begrudges the fact that her friends and family expect so much of her, even though that is precisely what she taught them to do. She secretly resents having to work so hard to make everyone happy. And the more she thinks about it, the more miserable she feels.

Self-righteous Rebecca

Rebecca is a modern-day Joan of Arc. In her teens, against the advice of her parents and her pastor, she married a good-looking, extremely charming young man who turned out to be an abusive alcoholic. Eventually, to compensate for her foolish mistake, Rebecca returned to the church of her childhood where she was regarded with admiration as the long-suffering wife of an unbeliever.

Because her selfish husband couldn't hold down a job, Rebecca was forced to go to work to support herself and her children. Her spouse didn't give her a dime. What little money he did make, he drank up. For years, she worked her fingers to the bone to feed and clothe her family. Meanwhile, her husband never even lifted a finger, although he raised his fist fairly often!

Rebecca didn't intervene in his alcoholism or act to protect herself or her children from his abuse. She tolerated intolerable behavior for twenty-one years and did little more than complain. She had no idea that she was martyring herself and her daughters. Nor did she recognize that she was teaching them to wallow in worry (passivity), rather than protect themselves from maltreatment (proactivity). Thanks a lot, Mom!

Her daughters considered their parents' dysfunctional relationship normal, because it was all they knew. They memorized their mom and dad's repertoire of relationship behaviors—fighting, yelling, blaming, and shaming. They acted out their father's disrespectful attitude toward their mother and learned to mimic her mournful expression, self-pitying posture, and negative thought patterns.

Rebecca's girls expected to be abandoned and abused, and, so far, they've succeeded in finding boyfriends willing to oblige them. Oblivious to the fact that they're repeating a pattern established by the previous generation, they've become their mother and will doubtless marry men like their father.

Hopeless, helpless Harry

Harry's story is different, but equally traumatic. He was nine when his mother died. Devastated by her prolonged illness and premature death, Harry was starved for attention and affection. When his father remarried two years later, he was overjoyed. But his happiness was short-lived. His stepmother had three children of her own to take care of, along with Harry and his siblings. She didn't have enough time and patience to go around.

Harry caught the brunt of her frustration. An unbending woman with a sharp tongue, she was harder on Harry than she was on the other children. She never missed an opportunity to humiliate him. He sponged up her negative attitude and became a pain-riddled bundle of shame, sadness, and low self-esteem. These characteristics were carved into his personality. The impact was visible. As a schoolboy, he already had a whipped-puppy look about him.

To add insult to injury, Harry had a learning disability. He was dyslexic prior to the time when dyslexia was well understood by educators. His peers teased him relentlessly. His teachers accused him of not trying hard enough and assured him that he wouldn't amount to anything if he didn't buckle down. Harry's feelings of inadequacy and inferiority multiplied exponentially.

Somehow, he survived the psychological torment of childhood. During his senior year in high school, Harry met an accomplished, intelligent young woman named Martha. Sensitive to his wounded state, drawn by his neediness, Martha felt compelled to rescue him from his fate. A caretaker from her earliest childhood, she had a gift for rescuing and repairing people. With two alcoholic parents and five siblings, she played the role of a little mother in her family and played it well. Martha parented her brothers and sisters better than their parents did.

Harry was seduced by her maternal qualities. Following a brief engagement, Harry and Martha were married. The young bride swung into action immediately. Mothering was what she did best. Determined to help her husband achieve his potential, convinced that if *she* believed in him enough, he would come to believe in himself, she did her utmost to be a loving and supportive wife. The first time she questioned Harry's judgment, however, the honeymoon was over. He experienced her questioning as criticism and became disproportionately hurt and angry.

Having been taught in childhood to disdain himself, Harry drew everything Martha said from that day forward through a negative mental filter. Her comments reinforced his self-doubt. There was little she could say or do that didn't offend him. Martha coped by becoming more subtle and manipulative when she made suggestions, which he recognized immediately and resented immensely. It was downhill from there. He got mad—she got even. She got mad—he got even. As the adage says, "It takes two to tangle."

Rageaholic Roger

Abandoned at birth, Roger was adopted by a couple who desperately wanted a baby. But, in spite of the fact that he had been *chosen,* Roger felt like a castoff.

Because he was their only child, his adoptive parents focused all their hopes and dreams on him. He was overwhelmed by their unrealistic demands for perfection. Although he tried his best to measure up, he never quite managed it. Eventually, Roger began to identify himself as a failure and wove that perception into the tapestry of his character. To paraphrase the words of Susan Howatch, it spread like a stain across the texture of his personality.[1]

In adulthood, Roger's negative self-concept created serious problems. He couldn't handle anything that he perceived as a put-down. If his friends offered advice, he thought they considered him stupid and took offense. If his employers gave him instructions, he thought they were implying that he was incompetent and responded angrily. If his wife had an opinion that differed from his, he assumed she didn't respect him. And he raged at all of them in an out-of-control fashion. Everyone close to him was terrified of his anger. Roger lost four wives, numerous friends, and several jobs because he was so easily threatened. He didn't realize that his negative attitudes were pushing people out of his life and preventing him from achieving his goals.

Amazing Grace

Wife, mother, Junior Leaguer, and PTA president, Grace is the queen of all caretakers. She makes herself indispensable to everyone. Her pastor insists he couldn't get along without her. She cleans the church, types the bulletin, chairs the social committee, directs the choir, and leads out in youth ministries. Every week after church, she invites the guest speaker and all out-of-town visitors to her home for lunch. What a saint!

No matter what needs to be done in the church or community, Grace can be counted on to do it and do it well. Fortunately, she owns an SUV. Today she's picking up a dozen curtain rods and ninety yards of linen to make draperies for the youth chapel. As soon as she finishes sewing them single-handedly, she'll be looking for someone to nod sympathetically while she complains about her difficult lot in life. Grace's children are often required to fill this role. Almost every day they are subjected to a dramatic discourse on her current woes. Little wonder that they get frustrated every time their mother volunteers to take on another gargantuan task. How could she forget so quickly? Why does she keep going back for more? The kids have lost their ability to empathize.

Recently, when her teenage daughter seemed reluctant to attend another one of Grace's self-pity parties, Grace shamed her by saying, "Parenting is such a thankless job." The girl ran screaming from the room.

Common factors

Grace, Roger, Harry, Rebecca, and Patsy have much in common. They are hooked on unhappiness. Trained to think and act in self-defeating ways, they are addicted to misery and martyring (undue self-sacrifice). As strange as it may seem, they find meaning, identity, and value in being victims. This kind of martyring is not to be confused with healthy self-sacrifice, generosity, or respectful tolerance of other people's quirks. It is an entirely different matter.

Unhealthy martyring is a neurotic condition that involves extreme self-sacrifice and other self-demeaning, self-destructive behaviors which are (1) excessive, irrational, and out-of-control; (2) detrimental to the individual and his or her loved ones; (3) driven by unconscious motives; (4) repeated in the face of obvious negative consequences; yet somehow (5) the key source of meaning and identity to the misery addict.

"Clairvoyant" Patsy, for example, believes that her only real value lies in what she does for others. There's a hidden motive in her generosity. If people fail to applaud her good deeds, she's deprived of her fix. Harry's and Roger's unmet childhood needs have programmed them to look for motherly partners, but they can't tolerate being questioned or controlled, which are typical parenting behaviors. They want the nurturing but not the nagging.

Rebecca thinks the only way she can get attention is to be a victim. The payoff is the sympathy she gets. And Grace? Grace just wants recognition and will do almost anything to get it.

I understand all of these well-meaning folks. They're my people. I belong to the same club. I started getting high on misery at an early age. An ultra-responsible child, I grew old before my time. Proud of the fact that I took life so seriously, I couldn't understand how anyone could laugh and have a good time when half the population of the planet was starving or dying in earthquakes and floods. I had honed "sombriety" to a fine art by the time I was thirteen.

In 1997, I attended a class reunion, during which Virginia, a high school classmate, reminded me of a conversation we'd had forty years earlier in the second semester of our senior year. Having taken two college classes the previous summer and two more during the first semester, I was preparing to start college as a sixteen-year-old sophomore that fall, thus skipping the best years of my adolescence.

When I told Ginny my plan, she asked why I was driving myself. Her dad was a college professor, but somehow she knew that teenagers were supposed to have fun. She couldn't imagine why I was driving myself so hard, and I couldn't imagine doing any less. I informed her I was doing it because I *had* to. I had an internal imperative that insisted I finish college in three years to save my parents' money. I was already disregarding my physical health and social well-being for an inglorious cause.

My personal experience and the case histories mentioned above illustrate a simple point: many people have been schooled to think, believe, and behave in self-defeating ways by teachers, parents, and authority figures who unwittingly model hurtful attitudes and actions. They unconsciously communicate incorrect messages to children that the children, in turn, translate into negative, jaded views of themselves, of the world around them, and of the people in the world. If no one tells them otherwise, they develop a condition I call *addiction to misery*. Not a pretty picture, but decidedly not their fault, as we shall see.

Hope for Today

Recently I heard someone say that pain is inevitable, but suffering is optional. I didn't like the sound of that one bit! I disagreed with the statement because it interfered with my negativity. Up to that point, I had been firmly convinced that suffering was noble—virtuous. The idea that pain is inevitable but that suffering is optional blew a hole in my identity as a victim. Faced with the fact that I could not easily get rid of my attitudes and beliefs, I had no choice but to ask for help. I acknowledged that I couldn't do it alone. I found many wonderful sources of wisdom, strength, and encouragement when I reached out for help. One expert says that everyone has the ability to remodel or rewire their brain. Actually, I needed a complete brain transplant. I'm still working on that. Meanwhile, I'm stepping out of the victim role—one day at a time and by the grace of God.

Self-Study

1. What addictions or unhealthy dependencies do you think might have been present in your childhood home? Substance dependence? Compulsive eating? Workaholism? Sex or relationship addictions? Rageaholism?
2. Write a few lines describing how you were affected by the above situation(s).
3. Rewrite your description, making it as humorous as you can. Or draw a caricature of yourself as a child trying to cope with a difficult situation.
4. If you find yourself overwhelmed or distressed by the content of this chapter, do not read further. Take a break for a few days. Consider speaking to a trusted friend or therapist about your feelings.

---

1. Susan Howatch, *Glittering Images* (New York: Fawcett Crest, 1987), 131.

CHAPTER 3

Exactly What Is a Negaholic?

This is my depressed stance. When you're depressed, it makes a lot of difference how you stand. The worst thing you can do is straighten up and hold your head high because then you'll start to feel better. If you're going to get any joy out of being depressed, you've got to stand like this.

— Charlie Brown

Let me introduce you to one of the best negaholics I know—a gentleman named Ned. Married, the father of three children, Ned was the personification of well-disguised pain and misery when I met him. He was so depressed that if he had fallen into a ditch or an open grave and a passerby had started shoveling dirt on him, he wouldn't have moved a muscle to keep from being buried alive. Ned alternated between two emotional extremes: weeping pitifully and seething with rage. But only the people closest to him were aware of his drastic mood swings.

Throughout childhood and adolescence, Ned was systematically scourged—verbally and physically—by his parents and peers. Four ideas were implanted in his mind—you are ugly; you are stupid; you are worthless; and you are a failure. Ned incorporated these erroneous messages into his belief system.

Because his parents had eight children to support, Ned worked in the family business throughout childhood and well into adulthood without pay. He received free room and board but no salary—not even gratitude. This deepened his sense of worthlessness.

At the age of thirty-three, he met a woman at church and fell in love. After a short courtship, they were married. Emily, his wife, failed to notice that Ned had a self-esteem shortage so severe that everything she did to make him feel better about himself fell into a bottomless pit. He expected her to give him the sense of value he lacked, but his emotional deficit was greater than the national debt. Emily couldn't pay it off.

Because he felt so inadequate, Ned begrudged his wife's every accomplishment, and she was an extremely accomplished woman. In his mind, her successes magnified his failures. For that reason, he began to sabotage her efforts. He went so far as to interfere with her completion of graduate school by throwing away the schedule for her final exam when it came in the mail! Poor fellow. He didn't mean to be such a jerk. He honestly didn't. To understand his history is to understand his dilemma.

Although he was a very talented man, Ned felt inadequate. He needed a spouse who could compensate for his weaknesses, but he hated her for it, much as he hated himself. In order to bolster his sagging self-esteem, Ned began collecting grievances against Emily. His resentments grew to the point that they occupied his every thought. He became more and more querulous and self-absorbed.

Obsessed with faultfinding, Ned focused on Emily's shortcomings—both real and imagined. She responded defensively, and the two of them became embroiled in a deadly power struggle. Each felt compelled to prove the other wrong in order to feel right.

Not surprisingly, their children were caught in the middle of this covert war. A religious fundamentalist, Ned had always considered it his children's sacred duty to provide him with the respect he lacked, but because he didn't respect himself, his children found it difficult to respect him. The harder he tried to force the issue, the more unpleasant his behavior became, which further diminished their respect.

When did this self-defeating cycle begin? In childhood, Ned played the victim role to the extent that it became his very identity. Used and abused as a youngster, he continued to accept—even unconsciously invite—persecution as an adult. Somewhere along the way, he discovered that helping people bolstered his self-esteem. From then on, he took self-sacrificial behavior to the extreme, offering his skills to individuals and institutions free of charge, selling his considerable talents for little or nothing, while his family went hungry—literally. He volunteered to be taken advantage of, which diminished his sense of value even more. Ultimately, Ned got hooked on selling himself short to earn approval, even though this behavior was self-demeaning and self-destructive. He knew his family was being deprived materially, but he couldn't stop. He could not change his behavior.

Today, Ned is hopelessly hooked on unhappiness. He's a compulsive controller and a world-class victim and martyr. He is addicted to negative patterns of thinking, believing, and behaving that are destroying his relationships and threatening his life. Ned is held hostage by negative self-perceptions. The shadow of death hangs over him and beclouds the lives of everyone he loves. Exhausted by the ongoing power struggle, drained of emotional resources, he is spiritually bankrupt, and his family is deeply distressed. Worst of all, Ned is imminently suicidal.

This story is so heartrendingly sad that I hate to tell it. But situations like this are more common than most of us realize. There are many wounded souls such as Ned and Emily who are struggling with problems they didn't ask for and don't understand. And they will lose the battle if they don't get help. Tragically, the casualties will be their children.

The good news is that recovery is possible. I know hundreds of families that have been remarkably transformed, beginning with one family member who had the courage to change. The sixteen-year-old daughter of a high-profile church administrator wrote a Thank-you note to me a few weeks after her father went through the treatment facility where I work. This is what she wrote, "I have a dad now. For the first time in my life, I have a dad."

The roots of negaholism

How would you define *negaholism*? I consider it a habitual frame of reference—a deeply embedded mental filtering system—through which everything looks bleak. For people reared in the midst of addiction or abuse, such an outlook comes naturally. It's like second nature. Adults who have endured painful experiences as children and who have been unable to express their feelings openly have a truckload of backlogged emotions. These feelings get stuck in the pipeline.

Several years ago, I asked my then twenty-nine-year-old son, Kurt, to e-mail me a sizable file of photographs that he had scanned at my request. For some reason, I couldn't download the file when it came in. My little computer hummed and blinked busily for ten minutes, and then I received a message that said, "Shame on you—your file is too big."

I telephoned Kurt, who obligingly divided the file in half and resent the material. But I couldn't download the smaller files either. I didn't realize that the original transmission was still stuck in the pipeline, preventing new messages from coming through. When I deleted the offending file, it reappeared. I still couldn't open it. I deleted it again and emptied the trash. Assuming that it was in the garbage truck going down the road, I logged off, triumphant.

When I logged back on, the original message was back. I deleted it yet again. It reappeared. I'm nothing if not persistent, but computers disdain persistence. I could not make that file go away. Being technologically challenged (would you have guessed it?), I had no idea what to do. Finally, it occurred to me to accept my powerlessness—my inability to solve the problem single-handedly—and call tech support. The technician said that my system was logjammed. The oversize file was too big to budge. That's why I couldn't get rid of it.

Negaholism is like that. Traumatic life experiences create painful feelings that build up and create a backlog of negative emotions that get stuck in the pipeline and recycle themselves endlessly. This may have to do with the fact that the brain itself has a bad-news bias. According to research done at Ohio State University, our brains react more strongly to negative stimuli than to positive stimuli. There is a greater surge in electrical activity when we hear anything downbeat than when we hear something upbeat.[1] Since our survival depends on our ability to detect and dodge danger, it's a good thing. But on occasion it can work against us. If the internal alarm system becomes hypersensitive and begins to cycle constantly, we've got a problem.

Why misery addiction is difficult to diagnose

Like alcoholics, misery addicts are the last to know that their behavior is problematic. Other people can spot their symptoms a mile away, but *they* can't. Negaholism is difficult to diagnose because (1) nobody *wants* to be miserable; (2) misery addicts don't enjoy being unhappy; (3) it isn't fun; and, in many cases, (4) they grew up in the presence of a victim or martyr—a parent or grandparent who griped and complained a lot—and they don't want to be like them. God forbid that they should ever become a whining, sniveling so-and-so like Aunt Eloise.

Co-misery addicts—people who grew up in the company of a negaholic relative—have an aversion to complainers. The last thing they want is to become one, which leads them to deny their own negativism. Unfortunately, they can't be anything *but* misery addicts, because children learn what they live with.

Remember that addictions hide in denial. Negaholism is no exception. It *isn't* fun. Whereas most addictions promise (and deliver) pleasure at first, misery addiction does not. When confronted by the habitual nature of their behavior, negaholics react defensively. "How can I be addicted to misery? I don't *enjoy* being unhappy!" True. They don't. But feeling crummy is familiar and therefore reassuring.

Leslie, a fifty-year-old aesthetician who is addressing her negaholism in therapy, made this ironic confession: "For years, I've complained about my *mom's* negaholism! I've literally made myself miserable over my *mother's* misery."

The nitty-gritty of negaholism

Negaholism is a profound addictive process that involves

- avoiding anything positive or pleasurable—otherwise known as *pleasure anorexia;*
- unconsciously seeking criticism, betrayal, rejection, guilt—anything negative or painful;
- attaching negative meaning to neutral or even positive events;
- being preoccupied with present and past insults;
- complaining to relieve uncomfortable feelings rather than taking

steps to address the problem that caused the discomfort in the first place.

Now, wouldn't you like to have this addiction? I ask groups of people suffering from various addictions and combinations of addictions (alcoholism plus a drug addiction plus an eating disorder, for example) if anyone would like to trade symptoms with a misery addict. No one has ever volunteered.

Pleasure anorexia

Misery addicts derive perverse pleasure from *avoiding* pleasure. The term *bulimiarexia,* which is self-starvation alternating with bouts of bingeing and purging, is an apt metaphor for misery addiction. Misery addicts starve themselves in the midst of social plenty and then binge and purge on complaining and sympathy-seeking. They settle for the crumbs of self-pity and being pitied by others, when they could be feasting on the nourishment of positive relationships. And they do it unconsciously. They may have a vague sense that something is wrong, but they don't know what to do about it.

Attraction to pain

The martyr's attraction to abusers is legendary. Would-be victims prefer to relate to bad guys, because nice, normal people aren't exciting. Inexorably drawn to bad guys or girls, misery addicts can't seem to figure out why their relationships always end in disaster. They can't imagine why the same things keep happening to them over and over again. Duh!

Some misery addicts are drawn to dangerous, painful, or stressful vocations or avocations, such as workaholism, perfectionism, compulsive overexercising, etc. Still others inflict pain on themselves by self-mutilation or by choosing partners who abuse them physically, sexually, or psychologically. Obviously, they don't do so consciously or deliberately.

Obsession with insults—real or imagined

Misery addicts are subject to a variation on Murphy's law: if anything *can* be misunderstood or misinterpreted, it *will* be misunderstood or misinterpreted. Remember the brain's negative bias? A good misery addict is capable of scanning a host of possible interpretations for someone's words or actions and coming up with the worst possible meaning in three seconds flat. Since negaholics have only a negative data bank to draw upon, this interpretation is inevitable.

At the peak of my martyring career, I went to a social event where I misinterpreted the hostess' greeting as a subtle statement of rejection. She had invited me to a picnic in spite of the fact that we'd been at odds recently. When I arrived, she greeted me by saying that the other guests were in the backyard. Assuming she didn't want to be in the same room with me, I took offense and huffed out to the backyard. Given my state of mind, there wasn't a thing she could have said or done that would have been OK with me. Frankly, I wouldn't blame her if she hadn't wanted to be in the same room with me, because I was so miserable.

Recently, someone misinterpreted *my* actions similarly. While teaching an adult education class one afternoon, I gestured randomly toward the left side of the room. Later, a student sitting on that side accused me of aiming my remarks at her. She felt betrayed. I couldn't have been more shocked. I've been guilty of greater crimes, but I was innocent on that occasion. At last I understood how my paranoia must have affected the people around me.

Ned, the negaholic husband and father mentioned at the beginning of this chapter, is a classic example of someone who assumes the worst. Harry and Roger, the macho martyrs described in chapter 2, automatically convert everything people say to them into an affront and then overreact. And Patsy, the compulsive caregiver, thrives on being unappreciated. It's nice to know that I'm not alone in my shameless, senseless self-pity!

Futile complaining

Fred has developed a habit of leaking anger out passive-aggressively at work. He complains to other employees about his colleagues' faults, rather than speaking to the persons involved. Complaining to a third party reduces the intensity of his repressed feelings just enough to prevent him from addressing issues directly. He wastes so much emotional energy while he's griping that he can't mobilize enough assertiveness to take care of the business directly and in a timely way. Griping and complaining to his peers instead of standing up and speaking to the principal party involved is part of Fred's ongoing problem.

Cassie, married to a sex addict for sixteen years, made the same mistake. Here is how she describes it:

> In the face of my husband's addiction, my backlogged emotions grew more intense with each passing day—like steam building up in a pressure cooker. As a good Christian wife, I thought it was wrong to gossip or complain about my husband. But the pain and anger inside me were slowly destroying my life.
>
> When I couldn't stand the stress any longer, I would look for a godly woman to confide in and pour my heart out. She would offer empathy mixed with prayerful counsel. Afterward, I felt better. These sessions depressurized the intensity of the immediate crisis. I came away relieved, resigned, determined to grin and bear the same insanity as before. So I returned to the battle for another round, proud of myself for finding a way to continue living with this intolerable situation. Over the course of our marriage, this scenario played itself out over and over.

Misery addicts who run around venting their frustration to sympathetic listeners may not realize it, but by defusing their feelings in this manner, they are dissipating the energy needed to create changes that might correct the situation that has caused their distress in the first place! Sooner or later, they have to decide how much energy they want to expend on futile complaining. Perhaps they could channel some of that energy into creative problem solving or healthy boundary setting, instead. But that would be too easy and effective. Remember Charlie Brown's advice: "If you're going to get any joy out of being depressed, you've got to stand like this."

In the chapter that follows, we will see how martyrs act out their addiction to misery. Brace yourself. This isn't going to be pretty. Meanwhile, arm yourself with the clear knowledge that no one, no matter how down in the mouth, wishes a misery addiction upon himself or herself. People come by their negaholism naturally. For that reason, they deserve a great deal of empathy and human respect.

Hope for Today

I saw a book title once that proclaimed the fact that happiness is a choice. *It may be an option for some people,* I thought, *but for me, it's not. There is no point in trying to be cheerful!* I knew how to make myself abjectly unhappy, but I didn't know how to conjure up a positive attitude. Eventually I found a group of people who understood how it felt to be trapped in "negativity city." They didn't beat me up for being so negative. They assured me that change was possible. And they were right.

Self-Study

1. Can you see how early circumstances over which Ned had no control shaped his character? List three positive traits and three negative traits that he developed as a result of early influences in his life. How does Ned's experience compare with your childhood situation?

2. Think of an occasion in your childhood or youth when someone's attention and approval made you feel good about yourself. Try to recapture that feeling and enjoy a moment of gratitude for the person who gave you that gift.

3. Celebrate the positive. Make a list of five to ten of your most admirable traits.

4. Eliminate the negative. Visualize someone who, either by word or action, diminished your value. Write a statement to refute that person's opinion or action. For example, "When I was five years old, you told me that I was bad news, Uncle Harry. You were wrong. I am a kind, helpful, generous person." Or, "When you told me that I would never amount to anything, Mr. Black, I believed you. But you were wrong. I am a worthwhile person."

---

1. Hara Marano, "Our Brain's Negative Bias," *Psychology Today,* June 20, 2003.

CHAPTER 4

What Martyrs Do Best

I have yet to see any problem, however complicated, which,
when you looked at it the right way, did not become still more complicated.
— Paul Anderson

There's a character in the Winnie the Pooh tales that is *negativity* personified: the pessimistic little donkey, Eeyore. Eeyore is the prototype for addiction to misery. He looks at the bleak side of everything. If there's going to be a picnic, he expects it to rain. When the wind blows, his house is sure to collapse. If there's a party in the Hundred Acre Wood, he won't be invited. He doesn't deserve good things. He isn't worth much. And on and on. Eeyore never runs out of things to be unhappy about.[1] Nor do other misery addicts.

Let's take a look at the martyr's modus operandi.

Assuming the worst

Assuming the worst is what martyrs do best. They await disaster, anticipate unhappiness, expect abuse or abandonment, and assume that everybody is against them. They know exactly what other people's motives are because they have an uncanny ability to read minds. Unerringly. The problem is that they *believe* their assumptions and act accordingly. Big mistake! Antidote: Stop trusting your thinking.

Absorbing blame and guilt

Most martyrs think they deserve to be maltreated, and, when it happens, they blame themselves. Then they obsess about what they did to cause the abuse, in order to figure out how to avoid repeating their mistake. This places them at the mercy of offenders and keeps them stuck in the cycle of physical and verbal violence.

Abusers are always glad to blame the victim in order to justify their own wrongdoing. Victims can never get it right, but they keep trying. Their willingness to accept blame and continue seeking approval (begging for crumbs from the master's table) are the very things that attract bullies to them in the first place. Savvy abusers know that a good victim will tolerate almost anything and never leave. Victims are held hostage to abusers by their guilt and fear of abandonment. This mindset is hard-wired into their brains at an early age. Here's how it happens.

When a youngster is abused physically or psychologically, the offender usually insists he or she did something to deserve it. The defenseless child accepts the blame and carries a burden of shame that doesn't belong to him or her.

A perpetrator who refuses to acknowledge the shamefulness of his actions has to place the blame somewhere. So he dumps it on his victim, who dutifully accepts it and begins to see herself as dumb, stupid, worthless, and defective. It's almost impossible to convince such individuals that they aren't dumb, stupid, and defective. Trust me. I've tried. Attempting to reason with a misery addict, in order to talk him out of his negative self-perceptions, is like trying to wrestle a football away from Peyton Manning.

Reenacting harsh "discipline"

Have you ever heard a group of childless adults speculating about the causes of juvenile delinquency in our society? They often declare that the lack of discipline is the culprit. Equating *discipline* with *physical punishment,* they theorize that if children were beaten more often, they would behave better. Research does not support this theory. In reality, the opposite is true. Harshness begets harshness! If *discipline* is understood as *disciplining*—teaching, guiding—then I would agree that children need more of it. But if it is considered punitive, I do *not* agree. I am convinced that punishing children violently and failing to guide them gently are the underlying causes of rage, violence, spouse and child abuse, addictions, and the victim mentality.

I should mention that the effects of verbal violence can be as profoundly damaging as the effects of physical violence. "Adult problems in self-perception and self-acceptance, relationship to others, and worldview can often be understood as the logical consequences of childhood maltreatment. . . . Much (if not most) of what we think of as adult psychopathology actually reflects long-term reactions to child abuse."[2]

We've established that many spouse and child abusers rationalize their behavior by accusing the victim of causing their anger. Even if a victim *does* trigger an abuser's rage, that doesn't justify battering! This is not to say that victims aren't responsible for their part in the problem if they've taunted a partner. Verbal provocation is not OK, *but it doesn't justify abuse as a response.* No one drives another person to act violently. And no one deserves to be abused, no matter how atrocious his behavior. Misbehaving children and misguided adults as well deserve gentle guidance and direction—not abuse.

By the way, the scriptural phrase "spare the rod and spoil the child" is alluding to the rod shepherds used to protect their sheep from wild animals. In my opinion, the biblical ideal is to protect children from threatened harm—not to beat them for their misdeeds.

Maltreated children often develop a victim mentality that is hard to get rid of. Misbehaving children need to be treated like innocent lambs— fiercely protected and gently and respectfully guided and corrected. A classic example of the irrationality of physical punishment is the adult who slaps a child to teach him not to hit his brother!

There's a vast difference between the unhealthy practice of beating children to discipline them and the healthy practice of setting clear boundaries and employing natural consequences to teach appropriate behavior. Sadly, the "shame on you, it's your own fault, you got what you deserve" excuse is a culturally acceptable alibi for child abuse in many social systems. Many victim or martyrs accept and recycle this attitude into their own child-rearing practices and thus perpetuate the problem.

Accepting the unacceptable and tolerating the intolerable

It's impossible to describe the frustration of the family of a misery addict. As I wrote in *Never Good Enough: Growing Up Imperfect in a "Perfect" Family:* "I've never seen rage like the rage of a child who has spent years watching his mother sit in the impotence of self-pity and whimper about the way her alcoholic spouse neglects his family. . . . She complains constantly, but she continues to tolerate intolerable behavior. She's like a doormat with a welcome sign emblazoned on it. Her position is painful, to be sure, but because it's all she knows, she accepts it as her due and does nothing to change it."[3]

Children who witness adults tolerating intolerable behavior learn to play the victim role. Acting as understudies, they imitate the victim's behavior and memorize his or her script. Thus, they are typecast in the victim role. Some improve upon the original actor's characterization—playing the part better than their model ever did, more skillfully and self-destructively, that is.

I believe that the birthright of every child is a place of safety and security in the world. Children who have not been provided with such a place assume that they must not deserve it—that they aren't worth protecting. This misconception becomes part of their worldview. The so-called victim mentality is fraught with such misapprehensions, none of which is easily shaken.

Worrying relentlessly

Misery addicts unconsciously seek out problematic circumstances to worry about. They make statements such as, "I'm worried to death," or "I'm worried sick." Now *that's* more than a metaphor! Evie, a nursing supervisor, shared an interesting tidbit with a colleague. "My mother repeated a sorrowful phrase over and over when I was a child: 'I'm down in the depths.' I'm having trouble freeing myself and finding relief from the habitually pessimistic attitude I 'caught' from her!"

Rehashing his worries reinforces the negaholic's pessimism. In some cases, he may have good reason to worry. The legitimacy of his problem isn't the issue. The issue is the extreme to which he takes his ruminating and the consequences thereof. Emotional distress creates anxiety, which registers in the body. Chronic anxiety is harmful to one's health. The more he "gerbils," goes round and round in his head trying to fix the problem, the greater the stress. And the greater the stress, the greater the anxiety. Careful, I'm getting dizzy!

One example of the mind/body connection is the well-recognized link between asthma and anxiety disorders. Columbia University researchers suggested recently in the *American Journal of Respiratory and Critical Care Medicine* that people who suffer from post-traumatic stress disorder are more than twice as likely to have asthma.[4]

Dr. Edward Hallowell, psychiatrist, author, and professor at Harvard Medical School, believes that worry can seize a person's brain and put him or her into a toxic trance.[5] An obsessive state is an altered state of consciousness.

People's fixations have a physiological basis. It begins when one part of the brain (the amygdala) senses danger and sends an alarm to another part of the brain (the prefrontal cortex). The prefrontal cortex starts analyzing the problem and creates a reverberating circuit between the two that is extremely difficult to intercept.[6] Yep, we misery addicts know all about that! We are caught in a cycle of discontent.

Anxiety has an adverse effect on our social well-being too. The higher our tension levels rise, the greater the likelihood that we will behave in self-defeating ways. Worrying puts people at their worst—not their best.

Normal individuals who recognize the futility of worrying manage to stop at a given point, but misery addicts *can't* stop. If they don't have something personal to fret about, they worry vicariously—obsess about someone else's problems. If they can't find anything in the immediate environment to be upset about, they'll settle for the president's morality, the pastor's grammar, or the condition of society in general.

Have you ever attended an old-fashioned negathon? When a group of martyrs get together to commiserate, they can spend enormous amounts of time and energy decrying the condition of society. I used to love this kind of communal worry fest. Now I retreat quickly whenever I hear anyone say, "What is this world coming to?"

The other day I was comparing notes with a few fellow misery addicts, when one suggested that we brainstorm about how to worry better. We created a master list of things to worry and obsess about so we wouldn't have to waste time generating new problems every day. See Appendix B for an "Exhaustive (and Exhausting) List of Things to Worry or Be Miserable About."

Grievance collecting

Martyrs never forget an insult. They can recount every detail long after the fact: day and date, what the offender was wearing, where he was sitting, and what he said. As suggested earlier, there's a biochemical explanation. When traumatic events occur, such as President Kennedy's assassination or Elvis Presley's death, our brains are flooded with chemicals that imprint details more deeply on the memory than "normal" traumas do. They are burned into our minds, sometimes creating "holes" that are almost impossible to repair.[7]

Most people remember precisely where they were and what they were doing when they saw the first media images of planes crashing into the World Trade Center. Some people register and record less dramatic experiences the same way.

Another reason misery addicts remember negative things so clearly is that they replay them over and over in their minds. Sandy made this confession to her Emotions Anonymous sponsor: "I obsess about all the awful things that have happened to me, until I feel so bad that I feel good." This insight came about as a result of her work in EA.

When she first joined, Sandy was a mess. Her husband of fifteen years had divorced her. Her children were rude and ungrateful. Her finances were a disaster. She was the laughingstock of her social circle. Ten months later, by the grace of God and with the support of her recovering peers, she is hardly recognizable as the bitter woman she once was.

The moment a martyr makes a new acquaintance, she can't wait to share her pathetic tale du jour. It's a habitual conversation starter. She fills lulls in the dialogue with complaints dramatized by appropriate sound effects—moaning and groaning, weeping and wailing. Her friends have heard her sob stories so often that they could recite them verbatim. Some develop a calloused attitude. When she starts to talk, they get glazed expressions on their faces and begin backing away.

Pam is a case in point. The minute she wakes up in the morning, she catalogs her aches and pains so she'll be ready to offer a detailed description to the first person she meets. At breakfast, she responds to her son's friendly "Whazzup?" with a groan. She didn't sleep well, she's exhausted, and the pain in her neck is worse. While eating her cereal, Pam obsesses about her to-do list. An unresolved problem attaches itself to the amorphous mass already rolling around in her head. Her face takes on a worried expression. As if on cue, her husband asks what's wrong. Pam launches into a litany of her woes. When she looks up, he has disappeared—and who can blame him?

A middle-aged housewife was betrayed by her mate. His infidelity was public knowledge. It wasn't as if anyone in the church or community was unaware of the scandal and needed to be informed. Yet his unfaithfulness was all she could talk about. Years after their divorce, she continued her campaign to discredit him. Her friends got so tired of hearing her rave about her ex-husband's sins that they began avoiding her. Her negative energy drove them away. Her attitude was even reflected in her appearance: she looked as if she'd been crossbred with a persimmon marinated in lemon juice.

Of course, we must acknowledge that betrayal can forever change the life of the person betrayed. Such individuals may reexperience the betrayal every day.[8] According to Dr. Hallowell, "When people are emotionally overwhelmed by an event, . . . they can never fully forget it or put it aside. It becomes impossible for them ever to 'get better' completely because their brains have been changed. The experience has branded them." However, he adds this helpful note: "The brain that has been changed in a negative way can change back in a positive way."[9] Thank God for that!

Renee, a stay-at-home mom, admitted to her best friend that she had developed a habit of saving up dramatic stories about the day's events to share with her husband when he came home from work at night. When she realized that everything she said was tinged with negativity, she decided to try sharing good news instead. "I found it almost impossible to be positive. I knew right then and there that I was hooked on unhappiness." Subsequently, Renee enrolled in a recovery program and is now one of the most positive people I know—a wonderful reminder that recovery is possible.

Attention seeking

Martyrs have a distinctive look about them. They wear pained expressions on their faces, their smiles look like grimaces, their foreheads are furrowed, their shoulders sag, and they have lots of migraine headaches. In his play *The Great White Hope,* Howard Sackler describes such individuals as "pinched up faces giving off the miseries."[10] If you've ever known a martyr, you may be picturing him or her right now and feeling slightly homicidal. Just kidding!

Inviting persecution

Martyr's minds are offense-seeking missiles. They don't feel right unless they're being wronged. They unwittingly set up friends, relatives, employers, colleagues, and even strangers to persecute them. Their agenda calls for the people around them to wrong them so they can feel right (think *familiar, therefore comfortable*).

Relating to misery addicts can be extremely difficult.[11] If you're a certified people pleaser, don't even *consider* marrying a martyr! Anyone whose self-esteem rests upon the approval of his mate will go bonkers in the company of a martyr because the only way to satisfy the martyr is to offend her. The only way to get it right is to be wrong. This is crazy-making. I've seen many partners of misery addicts puzzle over how they got roped into being the bad guy yet again. Eventually, they begin to doubt their own sanity.

Soliciting sympathy

Martyrs suffer in silence in order to elicit sympathy from others. Few realize that it's a ploy. Their behavior is so subtle that even *they* can't see it. Diane, a high school teacher, made this candid observation: "When I was active in my misery addiction, it was a constant challenge for me to arrange my face in such a way that others would notice my unhappiness and ask me what was wrong so I could complain with impunity." People who witness this kind of behavior unconsciously recognize that they're being manipulated and develop an inexplicable urge to go clean out the garage or organize their dresser drawers.

Feigning helplessness

Few misery addicts are able to ask directly for what they need. Instead, they find someone with the resources they require whether it be time, money, or skills, and stand as close to him as they can. Then they obsess in big outdoor voices about all their worries.

When Old Mother Hubbard notices that her cupboard is bare, rather than approaching someone who could help and asking directly, she whines loudly to someone else, "I just don't know what I'm going to do. My husband is out of work, and I served my last crust of bread for supper last night." If her act is convincing enough, the would-be benefactor will be reaching for his wallet before Old Mother Hubbard is halfway through her discourse. Most prosperous people are familiar with martyrs-who-lament. They say that if the downtrodden soul were to hold her head high and ask for what she needed without groveling, they wouldn't be annoyed. But when she assumes a defeated posture, positions herself near a potential benefactor, and obsesses out loud, the listener senses that he's being manipulated. This is demeaning both to the needy person and the designated giver. It's not shameful to be needy, but it's best to ask for help in a self-respecting manner!

Caretaking and then complaining

Some misery addicts feel compelled to rescue and repair others, to their own detriment, the detriment of their families, and even the detriment of the person they're helping! We call them *compulsive do-gooders.* Their benevolence wouldn't be so irksome if it weren't for the colossal complaining that follows. Complaining can be a subtle way of bragging. Martyrs overwork and then wear their weariness on their sleeves like a badge of honor. Patsy, the caretaker described earlier, and Grace, the all-too-familiar church lady, are prime examples.

Self-punishment, self-sacrifice, self-sabotage

Misery addicts are easily recognizable by their poor-me attitudes. They reek of paranoia and self-doubt. They berate themselves and use self-demeaning language. Some make a fetish of looking pale and wan. I call them "gray ladies." They sigh, look pathetic, act helpless, and neglect personal grooming. They judge themselves without mercy, beat themselves up, second-guess their own behavior, refuse to accept the forgiveness of God or man, suffer illness without seeking medical attention, fail to take care of their basic human needs, and expect others to take care of them. If this weren't so sad, it would be funny. Maybe I can see the humor in it now because I've begun to change. Obviously, the above description is a self-portrait. I am the original gray lady. You might have suspected as much.

Misery addicts have perverse ways of sabotaging themselves—cutting off their nose to spite their face. They procrastinate, refuse to set realistic goals, and fail to plan, thus thwarting their ambitions. They act out anger toward others by hurting themselves or by sacrificing themselves unduly, which is another form of self-punishment or self-neglect. Giving more than one can afford in terms of time, money, or effort is physically and emotionally suicidal.

When our sons were young, my husband and I sacrificed so much that they hesitated to ask for what they needed because they didn't want to add to our stress. While a self-sacrificial spirit can be an admirable trait, it can also mask egotism. Some compulsive do-gooders use people as objects on whom to practice their acts of virtue. So how do you know when you're doing this? We'll study the difference between healthy caring and unhealthy care*taking* in chapter 8.

Expressing feelings passive-aggressively

Negaholics leak their feelings out sideways in the form of passive-aggressive behavior. Derek, a young contractor, asked his wife, Terry, to run errands for him one afternoon when he had overcommitted himself to his clients. When Terry replied that she was too busy, he tried to solicit her sympathy. She didn't respond as desired, so he proceeded to accuse her of not appreciating the fact that the reason he worked so hard was for her sake. Terry *was* grateful, but she didn't have the time or energy to take on his burdens. Derek added snidely, "I would think a *loving* wife would care enough about her husband to help." Terry held her ground. Derek became verbally violent. When that failed to intimidate her, he upped the ante and began to push her around.

The methods Derek employed, in ascending order, were hinting, complaining, shaming, sarcasm, and physical violence. Since he had never been taught to do otherwise, it's little wonder that he used these tactics. He didn't know how to accept "No" for an answer without taking it personally. Taking things personally is a major symptom of misery addiction.

Unfavorable self-comparison

Comparing oneself with others is a guaranteed "high" for the nega-holic. Janis shared this dilemma with her Bible study group: "I developed the habit of comparing myself unfavorably to my peers at an early age. Obsessed with my appearance, I began to look at other girls competitively when I was ten. To this day, whenever I look at another woman, I compare myself to her. I think she's skinnier, prettier, better dressed, or smarter than me. I can't accept myself as I am and others as they are. I can't relate to them, because I'm so busy putting myself down!"

Janis's struggle is not uncommon nor is it confined to average-looking people. Note this remark by a well-known and very attractive actress: "I look at Liv Tyler and think, 'It's not fair,' because I can't find a flaw in her. And on top of that, she seems nice."

Martyring as learned behavior

Martyrs have no choice but to do what they do. Their negative attitudes, beliefs, and behaviors are learned at an early age and are deeply habituated. But change is possible. Mark, husband and father of three, is a testimony to that fact. Although he behaves reasonably well at work, he regresses into an immature, easily threatened adolescent at home. Why? When he was growing up with two actively alcoholic parents and a drug-addicted brother, Mark was badly abused and neglected. One expert says that children who aren't nurtured never grow up. Because, early on, Mark didn't have adequate nurturing and guidance, he remains an immature child in an adult body.

Eventually, he realized that his out-of-control behavior was setting a poor example for his children. He felt terrible about the stress he was placing on his wife. Afraid that she would lose patience and leave him, he sincerely tried to change but without success. In desperation, Mark called a therapist who urged him to go into a long-term treatment program to address his rageaholism. Following residential treatment, he continued with his outpatient counseling, twelve-step meetings, and a weekly anger management group.

Mark was willing to go to any lengths to break out of his negative behavior patterns. Inspired by his example, at least thirteen other members of his immediate and extended family have sought counseling or treatment and have begun their own journey to health and wholeness. Mark's personal healing is being passed along to the third and fourth generations. This illustrates something I have always believed: addiction and codependence are contagious diseases. But recovery is contagious too!

Hope for Today

I've had to wipe a lot of egg off my face when reflecting on my glory days as a misery addict. A skillful therapist taught me to laugh about it by having me say aloud, "I'm a mess, *ha-ha, ho-ho, he-he*" and continue repeating this until I burst into laughter. I pictured a caricature of myself running around begging people to let me take care of them so I could feel good about myself. I saw myself coming home at the end of the day so exhausted I looked like a wet alley cat that had just been in a fight. That mental image made me laugh *and* cry. Sometimes I would picture myself as an earnest little girl just trying to obey the rules. I would imagine myself picking up that child, sitting her on my lap, and telling her what a good little girl she was. Then I would assure her that she didn't have to work so hard to make me love her.

Self-Study

1. Review the typical behaviors of negaholics listed in this chapter. Make a list of your own martyring behaviors.
2. Go over your list and add the names of the person(s) who modeled this behavior to you. As you proceed, smile and affirm the fact that although you didn't choose to have negativity modeled to you, you can now change and grow.
3. This might be a good time to put *Hooked on Unhappiness* aside for a few days and integrate the facts and feelings the book has raised for you, especially if you are facing these for the first time. During this break, spend ten minutes every day journaling your feelings.

1. A. A. Milne, *Winnie-the-Pooh* (New York: Dell Publishing Co., 1974), 84–102.

2. Lucy Berliner, forward to *Child Abuse Trauma: Theory and Treatment of the Lasting Effects,* by John N. Briere (Newbury Park, Calif.: Sage Publications, 1992), ix.

3. Carol Cannon, *Never Good Enough: Growing Up Imperfect in a "Perfect" Family* (Nampa, Idaho: Pacific Press® Publishing Association, 1993), 125.

4. Amanda Gardner, "Vietnam Vets Study Links Asthma and PTSD," *HealthDay News for Healthier Living* Web site, http://www.healthday.com/Article.asp?AID=610052. (Accessed November 23, 2007.)

5. Edward Hallowell, 60.

6. Ibid., 59, 60.

7. Ibid., 64.

8. Edward Hallowell, 94.

9. Ibid., 64, 65.

10. Howard Sackler, *The Great White Hope,* quoted in Melody Beattie, *Codependent No More* (Center City, Minn.: Hazelden Foundation, 1987), 2.

11. See "How to Handle Chronic Complainers" in Appendix F.

Chapter 5

The Making of a Misery Addict

People get so in the habit of worry that if you save them from drowning and put them on a bank to dry in the sun with hot chocolate and muffins, they wonder whether they are catching cold.
— John Jay Chapman

How do misery addicts get so negative? Who programs them to be victims? As a society, we're beginning to understand alcoholism, but we don't have a clue about *negaholism*. Hooked on *unhappiness*? Are you crazy? It's not fun. It doesn't feel good. Drinkers reach for a second shot of whiskey because the first was pleasurable, but negaholism isn't pleasurable. Or is it? Could feeling *bad* make some people feel *good*? That is, in fact, the case.

Recent research into the workings of the human brain suggests a biological explanation for chronic negativity. Every time a martyr or misery addict punishes herself, she releases opiate peptides into her system—a full-force adrenaline rush that feels wonderfully awful, ecstatically agonizing.[1] We've known for some time that biochemical factors contribute to a person's vulnerability to alcoholism. Now we know that the same is true of negaholism.

Does this mean that misery addicts are doomed to remain unhappy for the rest of their lives? Not at all. People always have the ability to remodel their brains, according to Dr. John Ratey, clinical professor of psychiatry at Harvard Medical School. We are not prisoners of our genes or our environment. Rewiring the human brain is possible throughout life.[2]

We don't get to victimize ourselves either because of our heredity or our family history. Whether Mother Nature played a trick on us or the fates conspired against us, we can't use genetics or environment as an excuse to remain miserable today! We can and must go to whatever lengths are necessary in order to recover.

The evolution of negaholism

Social learning contributes to negative thinking habits. There are several ways to create a mini-misery addict: (1) model anxiety and negativism to a child when he or she is young; (2) fail to demonstrate healthy boundary setting, thus teaching him to victimize himself by default; (3) abuse or neglect him physically and emotionally; (4) sabotage his self-esteem by shaming him unduly; and (5) expect him to take second place to parental obsessions, compulsions, or addictions. Let's examine these five variables.

Role modeling

When children have a parent or grandparent who models extreme or unhealthy self-sacrifice, they learn to sacrifice themselves unnecessarily. Compulsive do-gooders derive meaning and identity from taking care of everyone but themselves—often to their own detriment and the detriment of their loved ones. They consider their excessive caretaking normal and necessary and cannot do otherwise, especially if they think good behavior is the ticket to success, riches, or eternal life. I speak as one who knows!

Here's an anecdote from my personal book of errors. Years ago, I set out to rescue an alcoholic single-handedly when she was extremely drunk. Bad idea. When she called me from a bar several miles away, I went to pick her up. The young woman was so inebriated that, on the way home, she tried to leap out of the car while I was driving fifty-five miles per hour. I had to wrestle to keep her inside. My car was weaving all over the highway, even though the passenger—not the driver—was drunk.

At that time, my sons were still young. I placed my life at risk without regard for my own safety or the well-being of my children, who would have been orphaned if the worst had happened. My behavior was foolish and reckless. Did I learn my lesson? No.

The first time this occurred, my naïveté might have been excusable, because I knew very little about the effects of alcohol. But when the same thing happened again, I had a better idea of what to expect. Nevertheless, I again went alone to rescue the inebriated woman. And I got the same results. Fool me once, and it's shame on you. Fool me twice, and it's shame on me!

Because martyrs have been schooled to hurt *themselves* in order to help *others,* they persist in rescuing and repairing people even when they realize that they or someone close to them could be harmed. Afraid that they will forfeit their right to exist in the present or to receive their eternal reward if they do any less, they soldier on. They are taking a positive biblical concept, being willing to lay down one's life for another, to an unhealthy extreme. This is how addictions are born.

Penny's family is a classic example. Her missionary parents sacrificed themselves for a cause they truly believed in. Their sincerity was unquestionable. Penny spent her childhood living in primitive conditions in third world countries. In adulthood, she chose not to follow in her parents' footsteps. Married and the mother of four teenagers, she lives comfortably in a custom-built home in an exclusive subdivision. But Penny feels an odd sense of guilt for not living up to her parents' altruistic example. To compensate, she overextends herself doing charitable work. Overly busy and highly stressed, she is emotionally unavailable to her family. She doesn't have time for the people who matter most.

Weak or missing boundaries

Children understudy the helpless, hopeless attitudes of adults around them who complain about their lot in life but do nothing to change it. Thus modeled to be nonassertive, they evolve into bewildered adolescents who can't stand up and speak up on their own behalf. Their auras of uncertainty and indecisiveness attract people who will take advantage of them and assume the right to manage and control their lives.

Adolescents who are overprotected or oversupervised are set up to become helpless victims. Kim, a lovely coed from a prosperous family, was pampered and protected in childhood. Her parents made all her decisions. When she was in college, she was so dependent on them that she had to telephone home several times a day for guidance and support. Even though her mother and father didn't intend to infantilize her, Kim felt helpless and insecure. She had no confidence whatsoever in herself and her ability to make decisions. She was unarmed and dangerous.

Not surprisingly, Kim was unable to say No when someone offered her drugs. In short order she was fully addicted. To her credit, she didn't waste any time getting help. Kim has been involved in twelve-step programs for three years now and is not only clean and sober, but she is a confident, self-possessed young woman who is no longer dependent on people or on substances for meaning and value.

Physical or psychological abuse

When a child is directly abused or forced to witness the abuse of others, he learns to play both the victim *and* the abuser roles. He is schooled to mistreat people and allow them to mistreat him. Hank is a case in point. Physically abused as a toddler by a violent alcoholic father and sexually abused by a priest when he was thirteen, he adopted a victim posture. But he was full of rage. Shortly after he married at the age of twenty-two, Hank's anger began to leak out on the people close to him— first his wife and later his children. If they didn't yield to his every wish, he became verbally and physically violent. He rationalized his violence by insisting that his wife and children caused it by refusing to give in to his demands.

Hank's wife finally took out a restraining order. He insisted that in so doing, *she* was abusing *him*. Hello? How could Hank have come up with such an irrational rationalization? Here's how: while witnessing his drunken father beating his mother, he learned the abuser role. When watching his mother suffer in silence, he learned the victim role. Now he flip-flops back and forth from the victim posture to the abuser position in his closest relationships.

After one of his nasty outbursts, Hank feels bad for hurting the people he loves. If they avoid him out of fear or mistrust, he goes into a self-pitying mode, which is intended to solicit their sympathy. Once he has paid penance by bringing gifts and flowers and making heartfelt promises, he earns his way back into their good graces. Then he escalates into a cantankerous maniac again. This exemplifies the well-known "cycle of violence."

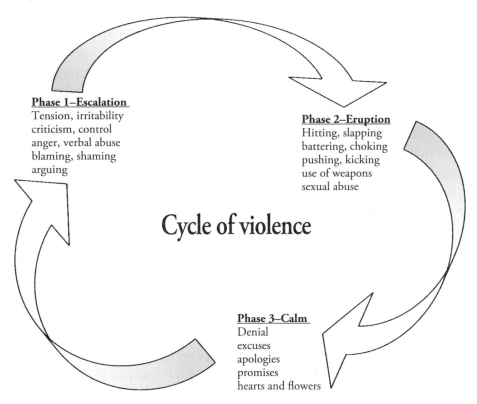

Phase 1–Escalation
Tension, irritability
criticism, control
anger, verbal abuse
blaming, shaming
arguing

Phase 2–Eruption
Hitting, slapping
battering, choking
pushing, kicking
use of weapons
sexual abuse

Cycle of violence

Phase 3–Calm
Denial
excuses
apologies
promises
hearts and flowers

Hank is a fortunate man. After taking out the restraining order, his wife went to a local agency that specialized in helping domestic violence victims. A counselor there suggested that she and her husband attend communications classes together and that they each see individual therapists. Several months later they went into couples' therapy with an experienced marriage counselor. In addition, they joined appropriate twelve-step groups, got sponsors, and worked rigorously on the steps. Hank has attended an anger management group twice a week for two years. The violence in their home has ended, and their relationship remains intact.

A self-esteem shortage

Most misery addicts were robbed of their sense of value at an early age. The undermining of their self-esteem may have been so subtle that they didn't recognize it for what it was. Some deny it completely. Others acknowledge that they were maltreated or neglected, but they don't connect that aspect of their history with the uncertainty and self-doubt they experience in the present. And they almost always make excuses for their abusers.

Allison's story is a good example, and it has a happy ending. As a young mother, Allison sensed that her children would not develop healthy identities if she didn't have a solid sense of her own personal value. A survivor of verbal abuse, Allison went to a counselor who used a well-established shame-reduction technique to help her expunge the demeaning messages ingrained in her by her father. In the process of regaining her identity, she also regained her sense of humor.

One day when she and her husband were looking through an old family photo album, they came across a snapshot of Allison and her dad taken when she was eleven. Allison commented with a chuckle, "That's Dad and me. He's chipping away at my self-esteem." By then, Allison was free of resentment. She knew that the shame her father had dumped on her belonged to him and not to her. It no longer dominated her life or dictated her self-concept. Yeah, Allison!

In some cases, the tendency to doubt ourselves comes from having unrealistic demands for perfection imposed on us as children. In perfectionistic environments, children are shamed for making mistakes. Since they can't be anything *but* human and thus imperfect, they feel defective when they make a blunder. In adulthood, they see even the smallest error as a sin punishable by death. Some adult children of addiction and abuse have been judged and criticized, poked and prodded to the point that there is nothing left of them but a peeled zero.

The addiction connection

In *Never Good Enough,* I wrote that misery addiction develops long before the negaholic marries a "persecutor" or gives birth to children who develop social and emotional problems.[3] Children of alcoholics and addicts grow up in the midst of lies, uncertainty, disappointment, broken promises, and shattered hopes. Their cuts and bruises are overt, visible. That type of dysfunctional family system *looks* dysfunctional.

Children reared in perfectionistic families face criticism, double standards, shame, and shattered spirits. Their wounds are covert, bloodless. This type of dysfunctional system *looks* functional. "Both the children of alcoholism *and* the children of perfectionism live in the land of fear and trembling. Their belief system is based on a single common premise: life is painful. This sets them up for addiction to misery."[4] The legacy of negativism is handed down from generation to generation.

Back in the days when we lived in "Ozzie and Harriet" land, the world (and the TV screen) was black and white. We thought that alcoholism caused family dysfunction. Nonalcoholic families were fine and dandy, or so we thought. *Not.* Now we know that *any kind* of preoccupation or drivenness on the part of parents can result in the neglect or abuse of children.

Blaming and shaming are standard operating procedures in abusive systems, whether the focus is on alcohol or on a druglike process such as workaholism, perfectionism, sexaholism, or relationship addiction. For children reared in these kinds of environments, unhappiness is a way of life. "Feeling good, experiencing pleasure, expecting the best, looking at the bright side . . . are totally unfamiliar to them. They grow up waiting for the other shoe to fall. As heirs to a legacy of negativism, they are programmed to expect the worst. Often their very expectation acts as a self-fulfilling prophecy."[5]

The martyr mentality

Because of the way they have been programmed, negaholics believe that (1) everyone is against them, (2) everybody is talking about them, and (3) everyone thinks badly of them. They're convinced that they can read minds, but they never read anything positive into people's actions. Once again, *assuming the worst is what martyrs do best!* Friends and family grow weary of their unfounded fears and false assumptions. As a result, their worst fears are realized. They are abandoned.

Pessimistic filters

Remember Harry and Roger, the male martyrs described earlier? Consider their plight in the light of this statement: "A martyr's pessimistic filters give negative meaning to events that are neutral or even positive. The negative meaning he assigns to situations sets off an emotional chain reaction that activates whatever disaster he may have anticipated. Some martyrs are so addicted to feeling terrible that they will sabotage anything good that happens and turn it into a catastrophe."[6] This was true for Harry and Roger. They couldn't handle anything positive.

Then there was the woman who complained about her alcoholic husband's irresponsibility but continued to tolerate it. She needed a persecutor in her life so badly that she deluded herself into believing she couldn't survive financially without him, even though he was a financial *liability*. She was capable of doing the math, but she was so invested in maintaining her identity as a victim that she overlooked the obvious: an alcoholic who contributes nothing to the family physically, emotionally, or financially is not an asset.

Helpless-hopeless attitude

The martyr's mentality is characterized by a helpless-hopeless attitude. This mindset becomes so habituated that the person literally *cannot* break out of the victim role.

Most people are shocked by media accounts of women who accept flagrant abuse from their partners and do nothing to protect themselves or their children. They are appalled when they read about mothers who passively collude in the abuse of their own children by boyfriends or stepfathers. In all probability, such behavior is a by-product of relationship addiction combined with misery addiction.

Very few professionals recognize victim behavior as an addiction and treat it as such. Do you recall the single mother who made headlines a few years ago by drowning her children in a lake and then claiming they had been kidnapped? According to some reports, her boyfriend didn't want a partner who had children, so she altered her identity—that of being a mother—to please him. That's addiction.

Obsessive religious environments

Lynn grew up in a conservative religious family where she was told, both verbally and nonverbally, that she didn't count and that her needs weren't important. Nothing mattered as much as God and church. Her father, a pastor and college administrator, was revered by many. When Lynn was little, her mother told her in hushed tones that he was a *man of God.* Lynn and her siblings were not allowed to set foot in his study because he might be writing a sermon or praying. She knew better than to bother Daddy with her childish needs.

As an adult, Lynn still apologizes for bothering him when she asks for his attention. "My father had plenty of time, attention, and affection for everyone else, but he gave none to his own family," she says. When she graduated from the church-affiliated college where he worked, Lynn's father missed the ceremony even though his office was just across the campus.

A few months after graduating, Lynn married a classmate named Danny. Determined to have a model Christian home, she was shocked to discover that her handsome husband had a violent temper—something he had hidden successfully while they were dating. When Danny began beating her, Lynn told no one. Eventually, she turned to her father for counsel, who impatiently exhorted her to forgive her husband and to try to be a better wife so he wouldn't have to hit her again! Excuse me? This is your *daughter,* sir!

Lynn sensed that the family's reputation in the community was her father's greatest concern. He seemed more worried about how he would look if her marriage ended in divorce than he was about her safety. Whether he intended to or not, he sacrificed Lynn on the altar of his ego. He preferred to have her risk her life rather than tarnish the family image.

In the Old Testament, entire nations were condemned because of their practice of sacrificing innocent children to idols. Lynn was sacrificed to her father's addictive religiosity, which, in this case, had become an idol. Lynn's father insisted that because she had made her bed, she must lie in it. That's exactly what she did until she developed suicidal depression and turned to a compassionate psychiatrist for help. By God's grace, she was spared.

Alcoholic environments

Kate's environment was similar to Lynn's, but the addiction in her home was alcoholism rather than churchism. Kate spent her childhood taking care of her mom every time her dad beat her up. She bandaged Mom's wounds, put her to bed, and took her to the emergency room on numerous occasions. Eventually her parents divorced.

You can imagine Kate's frustration when her mother married one batterer after another—five in all. When Kate finally sought professional help to deal with her own pain and anger, her mother was in the midst of her last divorce. Kate altered the course of her future by getting professional help. Her mother eventually checked into treatment as well.

The impact of addiction and abuse

Two-year-old Lisa was left in the care of a male cousin while her parents were at work. They had no idea that he was sexually molesting her. When she showed signs of emotional distress, they never even considered the *possibility* that she was being abused. Abuse was not even in their frame of reference. Unprotected as a toddler, Lisa was set up to accept further abuse. When she was raped as an adolescent, she didn't know it was OK to resist, cry out for help, or ask anyone to protect her.

By age thirteen, she had been molested by a teacher, a neighbor, and another relative. The long-range impact of these events nearly cost Lisa her life. Until she got professional help in her thirties, Lisa suffered from depression, anxiety, anorexia, and a disorder of sexual desire. Similar examples of childhood neglect and abuse could be given for families in which other "clean" addictions are practiced, including gambling, compulsive spending, relationship addiction, and Internet addiction.

I once saw a cartoon depicting a dejected-looking, Linuslike toddler standing in her daddy's home office with her thumb in her mouth and her blankie trailing behind her. She was waiting patiently for her daddy to notice her while he was staring, transfixed, at the computer monitor in front of him, saying, "Honey, don't bother Daddy when he's in his chat room!"

To choose or not to choose

Did Lisa, Kate, and Lynn, *want* to be victims? Did they *choose* to become misery addicts? I think not! But until they received medical and psychological help, they had no other alternative. *If there's only one option on the ballot, there is no real choice!*

By definition, compulsion is behavior without conscious choice, behavior that bypasses the rational mind and responds to mandates or unholy commandments learned in childhood, behavior so automatic that the individual does it without thinking.

When addictions of any kind—chemical or nonchemical—are present in a home, children are hurt. They develop a negative, pessimistic worldview. Most misery addicts learned to victimize themselves as a result of having been involuntarily sacrificed in childhood for the sake of someone's obsession, addiction, or untreated mental illness. By way of illustration, here is a so-called Russian joke that's not at all funny.

Son: "Father, now that vodka is more expensive, will you be drinking less?"

Father: "No, my son, but you will be eating less."

The neglect of a child's basic physical or emotional needs is typical of addictive environments. This is common to *all* addictions—not just chemical dependence. The greater tragedy is that when the children of addiction and abuse develop relationship problems or addictions of their own in adulthood, society blames them. And they blame *themselves*. They don't realize that they were cast in the victim role as children and thus programmed for self-destruction. They don't know that they have any other option, and they don't think it's OK to ask for help. They don't believe they deserve to *live*—let alone ask for help. No wonder so many victim-martyrs try to end their misery by ending their lives!

Today, we know there are other alternatives. When misery addiction is treated as a primary, chronic, progressive, and potentially fatal illness using a therapeutic approach that includes twelve-step programs, counseling, and medical intervention (if indicated), high-quality recovery and healthy relationships are possible. I'll vote for that!

Hope for Today

In our "pull yourself up by your own bootstraps" society, many people think that because we can't change the past, we should just put it behind us and move on. Hence, there are scores of adults whose childhood wounds lay deeply buried inside, affecting them in ways they know not. These individuals need a compassionate friend who can assure them that they didn't cause their abuse, that there wasn't anything they could have done to prevent it, that it wasn't their fault, and that they didn't deserve to be hurt—nor do they deserve to continue suffering. Why is this kind of comfort so hard to give and receive? It is readily available in places like Al-Anon, Adult Children of Alcoholics (ACoA), Emotions Anonymous, and Co-Dependents Anonymous (CoDA). In my own experience, being free to grieve my losses and feel genuine *sorrow* for myself has helped me to abstain from feeling *sorry* for myself (self-pity).

Self-Study

1. Make a list of the people around you when you were growing up who were sad, depressed, or obviously worried. What percentage of the time were they unhappy? Did they do anything to change their circumstances? Or did they just complain?

2. In your childhood, did anyone close to you hurt themselves to help others?

3. Did anyone tolerate intolerable behavior—accept the unacceptable? How did you feel when witnessing this?

4. To what extent do you think these individuals influenced your beliefs and behaviors?

---

1. Chérie Carter-Scott, "Do You Live or Work With a Negaholic?" Negaholics.com, http://www.negaholics.com/live_with_a_negaholic.html.
2. John Ratey, *A User's Guide to the Brain,* 17, 36, 38.
3. Carol Cannon, *Never Good Enough,* 123.
4. Ibid.
5. Ibid., 124.
6. Ibid.

CHAPTER 6

Brain Chemistry for People Who Don't Have Doctorates

When confronted by a difficult problem, you can solve it more easily by reducing it to the question, How would the Lone Ranger have handled this?
— Brady

The original title of this chapter was "Brain Chemistry for Dummies," but I changed it because I didn't want to feed anyone's addiction to misery. *You* should try writing a book about misery! How about an optimistic thesis on pessimism? *Smile.*

We're going to study the relationship between brain chemistry and chronic negativity now. I'll try to describe it in a way that people who don't have doctorates can understand. If I do this awkwardly, it's because I don't have an MD or PhD either.

For more than twenty-five years experts have been aware that there are biological underpinnings to various kinds of social and emotional distress.[1] "From the habitual worrier who torments himself by incessantly searching for what can go wrong in life, to the survivor of a traumatic past who is unable to let go of the pain, to the self-castigating perfectionist who lives in major fear of even minor failures, excessive worriers abound in all stations of life," says Dr. Edward Hallowell, coauthor of *Driven to Distraction.*[2] Researchers have pinpointed what is taking place in the nerve cells of the chronic worrier. They know what neurotransmitters might be to blame and what remedies might quiet the storm.[3]

Our operating system

The brain's job is to process data, make value judgments, formulate goals and plans, process decisions, store memory, generate recall, fuel creativity, and keep a person's bodily systems running automatically. To the extent that an individual's hard drive has been miswired or his software misprogrammed, his thinking is distorted. Garbled images appear in the mind, like the gobbledygook that shows up on a computer monitor when you click the wrong button. Scrambled thoughts produce scrambled feelings—emotional gobbledygook.

Most computers have pop-up blockers, firewalls, virus protection, and other mechanisms to report and repair problems. But mental computers don't. We can't check the hard drive in our heads, troubleshoot problems, uninstall and reinstall software, scan for viruses, add security devices, increase memory, or update peripherals. Wouldn't it be great if we *could*? Excuse me while I delete my obsolete messages, remove my temporary files, and defragment my brain. It will take only a minute.

Brain chemistry 101

With my apologies to scientists and techies for oversimplifying a complex mental ecosystem, I'd like to compare the human brain to a soggy computer in which electrical messages are transmitted through fluid-filled bubbles. I realize that this is a sloppy analogy from a neurochemical standpoint, but it will do for now.

The chemical messengers in the human brain are called *neurotransmitters.* The brain's ability to function is based on the presence or absence of these substances and how well they are balanced. Anxiety and depression result from imbalances. You may recognize the names of some of the most commonly known endorphins or chemical messengers: serotonin, dopamine, and norepinephrine. Surges in these chemical messengers determine a person's moods and his susceptibility to addiction and emotional upheaval.

The brain's operating system is fairly delicate. Messages speed down the threadlike part of a brain cell called an *axon* and are carried by the neurotransmitter to the threadlike part of another brain cell, which then "receives" the message. A person's mood is affected by the quantity and combination of chemicals present and by the amount of time they remain in the space between brain cells before they are reabsorbed by enzymes designed for that purpose.

Drugs of abuse affect these variables, as does early life trauma. Childhood trauma can permanently lower the brain's production of serotonin and render a person more prone to negativity, depression, impulsivity, and even violence. Such individuals benefit greatly from professional help, as do the people around them. If the threat of violence exists, one should not hesitate to get help. Anyone who is a danger to self or others needs immediate medical attention.

Cranial anatomy

The brain is divided into five segments, each specializing in handling various thinking and feeling processes. These segments are the limbic area, cingulate gyrus, amygdala, frontal lobe, and basal ganglia. According to experts, many difficulties associated with anxiety, depression, extreme social sensitivity, and excessive worrying are related to these five brain systems. When they aren't functioning properly, people can't handle their emotions very well.

Dr. Daniel Amen, clinical neuroscientist, psychiatrist, medical director of a behavioral health clinic, and author of *Change Your Brain, Change Your Life,* says that the proper working of one's brain determines how happy he is, how effective he feels, and how well he interacts with others, including God.[4] Notice this incredible statement: "Without optimal brain function, it is hard to be successful in any aspect of life, whether it is in relationships, work, schooling, feelings about yourself, or even your feelings about God—no matter how hard you try."[5]

Originally oriented to the idea that stressful early beginnings can create lifelong problems, Dr. Amen now believes that people's emotional and social problems are also related to the physiology of the brain. Until recently, because of the lack of advanced tools for studying brain function, we could only speculate about the brain's role in personality problems. Today we know that there is hope for treating problems we once thought were all in our heads.[6]

Using nuclear medicine technology known as a SPECT scan (Single Photon Emission Computed Tomography), researchers have found evidence of brain patterns that correlate with both depressive and obsessive tendencies. They are learning more about the effects of substance abuse, head injuries, and even negative-thinking habits on the brain.[7]

Specific brain systems affect our moods and personality. People who struggle with moodiness and negativity often have problems in the limbic system—the part of the brain that sets a person's emotional tone. When this system is humming along normally, the individual feels positive and hopeful. But if it is heated up a few notches, negativity takes control.

"When the deep limbic system is inflamed, painful emotional shading results," says Dr. Amen.[8] This is the filter through which we interpret daily events. If the system is overactive, we are likely to interpret neutral events through a negative filter. If it's functioning normally, a neutral or positive interpretation is likely.[9] Underactivity and overactivity are mediated by our unique brain chemistry. Premenstrual syndrome (PMS) is a classic example of this emotional shading principle.[10] Who knew?

The deep limbic system is where people stash away highly charged emotional memories. The more trauma we experience in early life, the more negatively oriented we become.[11] (I love it when researchers validate my opinions!) Dr. Amen states that "pessimism actually could be a deep limbic system problem because, . . . when this part of the brain is working too hard, the emotional filter is colored by negativity."[12] When another area of the brain—the basal ganglia—is overactive, it creates anxiety and nervousness. And when the cingulate gyrus is overactive, people get stuck in certain patterns or loops of thinking and believing.[13] It's comforting to know that there are physiological reasons for our proneness to misery, isn't it?

People can enhance the brain's functioning by using cognitive exercises, nutrition, medication, social networking, and many other tools and techniques that are included in good therapy and twelve-step programs. Even if we are genetically predisposed to negativity, we can do something about it. Help is available if we're willing to reach out. To the extent that our ability to function is impaired, we must seek help from first-class professionals. That's a given.

John, a thirty-year-old computer geek who couldn't make relationships work because he had such a depressive nature, was unwilling to take prescribed medication because he considered it a sign of weakness. Now there's a double bind!

When John's negative emotions became so overwhelming that he began considering suicide, he went to his pastor for help. The pastor suggested that he have a thorough psychiatric evaluation and encouraged him to follow the doctor's recommendations whether or not he agreed with them. The doctor prescribed an antidepressant, which John reluctantly agreed to take. The medication helped him to break out of his negative thinking pattern and benefit from counseling. After two years in therapy, John is now tapering off the medication under his doctor's supervision.

Psychologist Daniel Goleman explains why medications are necessary in some cases:

> When one's emotions are of great intensity and linger past an appropriate point, they shade over into their distressing extremes—chronic anxiety, uncontrollable rage, depression. And, at their most severe and intractable, medication, psychotherapy, or both may be needed to lift them. . . . *It is possible for chronic agitation of the emotional brain to be so strong that it cannot be overcome without pharmacologic help.* For people with worries so severe they have flowered into phobia, obsessive-compulsive disorder, or panic disorder, it may be prudent to turn to medication to interrupt the cycle. A retraining of the emotional circuitry through therapy is still called for in order to lessen the likelihood that anxiety disorders will recur when medication is stopped.[14]

The environmental factor

With the right genes, the right environment, and plenty of practice, almost anyone can become a misery addict. Repeated often enough, long enough, and hard enough, negativism becomes compulsive. Take, for example, the misery addicts portrayed in chapter 2: Amazing Grace overdoes everything and then complains to anyone who will listen. She learned this behavior from her mother, who sacrificed her personal well-being and ignored her children's needs in order to keep her abusive husband out of jail.

Patsy, the compulsive caretaker, overcommits her time and energy and then feels sorry for herself—something she often saw her dad do. Rebecca, the co-alcoholic wife, accepts her spouse's drunken behavior, because she feels morally obligated to do so. Because she believes divorce is a sin, she sees no option but to accept his unacceptable behavior. A peer at church told her that if she dies as a result of being battered, she will have died for a noble cause—*and she believed the woman!* She didn't consider the possibility she could be dragging her daughters into her coffin with her.

If Rebecca had healthy intellectual boundaries, she would be able to assess other people's opinions and decide for herself what to think. Lacking such boundaries, she is unable to separate human opinion from divine mandate. Skills for healthy boundary setting can be learned in individual and/or group therapy.

Roger, who was adopted into a perfectionistic home, has trouble accepting guidance, because his self-esteem is lower than a snake's belly in a wagon rut. Harry, who was a scapegoat for his stepmother, overreacts to criticism. All of these individuals are hooked on unhappiness.

Negatively oriented relationships

Martyrs have subzero self-esteem. They have a shame core that won't quit. In the workplace, they experience instruction as an insult and criticism or correction as rejection. At home, they're impossible to please, because they don't *want* to be pleased—being satisfied would interfere with their misery. Imagine being married to any of the characters mentioned above.

Patsy and Grace never slow down long enough to feel their pain. They are so anesthetized by the highs they experience when they hurt themselves to help others that they don't know they're utterly exhausted. Their families have to settle for what's left after they've spent their best energies people pleasing and approval seeking. *Many compulsive do-gooders are driven to martyrdom, but few are called!*

Harry's and Roger's wives, children, friends, and coworkers walk on eggshells. If they say anything that could be interpreted in a negative way, they will be verbally or physically abused in return. They hardly dare ask an innocent question for fear it will be taken as an insult. Notice these typical exchanges in homes where martyrdom reigns.

Husband: "I had a hard day at work. I'm beat."

Martyr wife: "You think *I'm* not tired? I got up early to help Suzie practice for her piano recital. Then I drove the kids to school and shingled the roof before I went to Junior's soccer game *alone.*"

*   *   *   *   *

Husband: "Honey, did you pick up the dry cleaning?"

Martyr wife: "How was I supposed to know you wanted me to pick it up? I can't read your mind. I have other things to do, you know. Just because I don't have a job doesn't mean I don't work myself to death. I suppose you'll want me to remodel the chicken coop next."

*   *   *   *   *

Wife: "What's our bank balance, dear?"

Martyr husband: "Why do you want to know? Money! That's all anybody in this family cares about. I'm just a money machine."

*   *   *   *   *

Child: "Mommy, what's wrong?"

Martyr mom: "Nothing!" (*sob, sob*)

*   *   *   *   *

Child: "Mom, can we go to Billy's place to play?"

Martyr mom: "Absolutely not. You have to clean the house. Remember what happened the last time you didn't pick up your toys before Dad came home? He got mad and went to the bar and didn't come back for three days, and it was *your* fault."

Martyring as behavior without choice

Looking back on my heyday as a martyr, I know that I didn't *choose* to be miserable. My inability to be positive was not for lack of wanting to be. If a sincere desire to change had been enough to accomplish the transformation, I would have overcome my negativity in a heartbeat.

Martyrs don't *want* to be miserable, any more than people with colds wants to sneeze, or people with viruses want to vomit. People with colds sneeze because they have colds. Alcoholics drink because they're alcoholics. And martyrs are miserable because they are hooked on negativism and/or because they have a neurological predisposition to unhappiness—not because they're bad, stupid, or perverse.

If people learn what they live with, if more lessons are indeed "caught" than "taught," as educational psychologists theorize, then perhaps compulsion *is* behavior without choice—behavior that bypasses the rational mind and responds to unconscious mandates learned in childhood, behavior so automatic that we do it without conscious thought or intention.

If I have ever known *anyone* who didn't want to be the way they are, it's a misery addict. Yet they're powerless to change. This is actually good news. When we're convinced of our own weakness and stripped of all self-sufficiency, we're in a position to turn our will and our lives over to a source of wisdom and strength outside ourselves.[15] And that, my friends, is the ultimate solution.

Hope for Today

Powerlessness is empowering. Admitting our powerlessness allows us to stop trying to achieve the impossible—conquering our addictions single-handedly—and start doing what *is* possible, that is, reaching out to viable sources for help with a problem that is bigger than we are. Asking for help is not a sign of weakness. It is a mark of courage. It flies in the face of misery addiction. When misery addicts stop trying to achieve the impossible, they can muster the resources needed to fight their disease effectively.

Self-Study

1. Many misery addicts start thinking and behaving addictively or pre-addictively when they are young. In looking back on your life, try to remember the first time you risked hurting yourself to help someone else. Were you rewarded in some way?

2. Now try to recall the first time someone close to you suggested that you were being selfish when you asked for a legitimate need to be met. In what ways might your request have inconvenienced the adult who shamed you for being so needy?

3. Do children and adults have a right to express their legitimate needs and wants?

4. Can you comfort yourself now with the knowledge that your expressed needs were legitimate? At this very moment, allow yourself to feel empathy for the child you once were and express your feelings in a sympathetic letter to yourself as a youngster.

1. Edward M. Hallowell, *Worry,* xiv.

2. Ibid.

3. Ibid.

4. Daniel Amen, *Change Your Brain, Change Your Life: The Breakthrough Program for Conquering Anxiety, Depression, Obsessiveness, Anger, and Impulsiveness* (New York: Time Books, 1998), 3.

5. Ibid., 8.

6. Ibid., 3.

7. Ibid., 4.

8. Ibid., 38, 39.

9. Ibid.

10. Ibid., 39.

11. Ibid., 40.

12. Ibid., 43.

13. Ibid., 9.

14. Daniel Goleman, *Emotional Intelligence: Why It Can Matter More Than IQ* (New York: Bantam Books, 1995), 57, 58, 69.

15. See Ellen G. White, *The Desire of Ages* (Nampa, Idaho: Pacific Press® Publishing Association, 1940), 300.

CHAPTER 7

Marital Martyring: The Holy Mother/Bad Boy Syndrome

I think the most uncomfortable thing about martyrs is that they look down on people who aren't.

— Samuel Behrman

So the martyr or misery monkey is on your back. It shows up when you least expect it and starts chattering in your ear. *Yakkety, yakkety, yak.* Think about how negative self-talk influences your attitudes, which, in turn, affect your closest relationships. You can count on one thing: it doesn't improve them.

When I was in graduate school, I ran across a research paper on double-alcoholic marriages. The study addressed the question of why so many alcoholics marry other alcoholics. That does seem strange, doesn't it? The answer is simple: Alcoholics move in the same social circles. They hook up at parties, bars, and AA. Based on the law of averages, some fall in love (or codependence) and get married.

Experts say that sick doesn't attract healthy, and healthy doesn't attract sick.[1] Everything within me rebels against this notion (could I be taking it personally?), but it's probably true. If sick doesn't attract healthy and healthy doesn't attract sick, then alcoholics or otherwise emotionally unavailable people will be drawn to alcoholics or otherwise emotionally unavailable people. Hence, the double-alcoholic, double-workaholic, or double-negaholic relationship. Consider the possibilities when you mix and match!

It's a well-known fact that, in a room full of people, if only two are dysfunctional, they will zero in on each other with unerring accuracy. They have subconscious radar. *Zap, bam, boom.* Love at first sight. Some enchanted evening, the eyes of two wounded people meet across a crowded room, and the fireworks start. The courtroom battle comes later.

So alcoholics meet each other at bars and parties and AA meetings, and misery addicts meet at Al-Anon or CoDA or church or the gym. The end result? A double-martyr marriage. Misery addicts are attracted to other misery addicts and to anyone else who can make them miserable. Who can accomplish this better than a full-blown alcoholic or drug addict?

Misery addicts make fabulous enablers for alcoholics and addicts. *Enabling,* in the context of addiction, is helping someone stay sick—doing everything necessary to perpetuate his or her addictive behavior. Martyrs are a drunk's dream. They pay the alcoholic's or addict's rent, buy him cars, bail him out of jail, pay his alimony, loan him their credit cards, etc.

One-downsmanship

Once two misery addicts have made their relationship official, they get right down to business. Now it's a competition—each vying for the one-down position! Why? Because when they're *one-down,* they feel *one-up.* To the extent that it is manipulative, being pitiful can be very powerful.

Since no two martyrs are exactly alike, their symptoms don't have to be identical for them to be equally addicted to misery. Both will manifest their symptoms in such a way that each is able to convince him or herself that the other person is sick, sick, sick, but *he* or *she* is just fine! Thus, the "Beauty" and the "Beast," the "Goodster" and the "Badster," "Holy Mother" and the "Bad Boy," "Father Divine" and the "Evil Daughter" or "Stepdaughter."

Unaware that they're stuck in an addictive cycle, each maintains a self-righteous attitude toward the other. The wife convinces herself that she is superior to her partner in order to escape the pain and shame of her own victimization. People who rigorously defend their *rightness* do so because they feel defective and worthless. They *have* to be right or they will crumble into a million pieces. Martyrs fear being wrong so much that they would rather die than admit a mistake. They're convinced that you or I or God will reject them if they admit their fallibility.

Those of us who can't accept our humanity end up isolated and alone, because it is in sharing our humanity that we connect with others emotionally. It is our blunders and quirks that others find charming—not our flawlessness. The martyr's self-righteousness creates the very thing he or she fears most. He or she ends up alone in the middle of the universe.

The shame-on-you syndrome

Double-martyr marriages rapidly deteriorate into mutual blaming societies. Trying to manage and control one another's behavior becomes the dominating feature of the relationship. Each partner compares the other unfavorably to himself. Then, from a position of great superiority, each focuses on fixing (controlling) the other. It's an earthshaking power struggle. In some cases, the adrenaline generated by the battle becomes addictive in itself.

Several misapprehensions fan the flames. Both martyrs are convinced (1) that the other doesn't *really* love them; (2) that their needs aren't being met and probably *never* will be; (3) that if their partner really cared, he or she would be able to read their minds and grant their every desire, perfectly, at all times; (4) that *they* are getting the short end of the bargain in the relationship; (5) that they are putting forth a great deal more effort than their partner is—which, of course, the partner doesn't appreciate in the least; and (6) that they are better at sacrificing themselves than their spouse could ever be. In other words, "I am holier and nobler than thee. Woe is me!"

Self-pity city

In double-martyr marriages, both partners are as saturated with self-pity and self-loathing as a dirty sponge in a mop bucket. Even though they are each responsible for generating their own feelings, both believe that the other person is *making* him or her feel the way he or she does. Lacking emotional boundaries, each blames the other for his or her pain and problems. Let's eavesdrop on a typical martyr's way of complaining about his or her spouse.

Wife: "I've *tried* to tell my husband how I want to be treated, but he won't listen."

Husband: "My wife won't let me do *anything*. I'm a prisoner."

If that's the case, then he might be wise to rethink the relationship. But if he did that, he might decide to end it and thus lose his persecutor. Then there would be no one to blame for his misery! So he stays for the sake of the children.

* * * * *

Here's another example. Wife (spoken sarcastically): "It's OK for *him* [spoken with disdain] to do such-and-such, but it isn't OK for *me*. What's good for the gander isn't good for the goose." Again, a healthy person would probably do something about the double standard rather than just complain about it, but not a martyr. Martyrs savor their misery too much to do anything to resolve the issue that's making them so unhappy.

* * * * *

Wife: "He never listens to me. Everything I say goes in one ear and out the other."

Husband: "I get so tired of her mindless chatter that I just turn it off."

* * * * *

Wife: "He always defends his parents [sister, ex-wife, children by a previous marriage] instead of me. He never takes my side, never stands up for *me*."

Husband: "She's a big girl. She needs to learn how to take care of herself."

* * * * *

"My husband considers me stupid because I didn't finish college. Why does he think I dropped out? I dropped out so I could work full time to pay his way through medical school!"

"My husband and children don't appreciate anything I do for them."

"My wife thinks she's my mother." Or, "My husband treats me like a stupid little girl."

"What does a man have to do to get some respect around here?"

"I always have to tell him what needs to be done around the house. Why doesn't he take responsibility? I'm sick of having to remind him all the time. But if I didn't, nothing would ever get done. *[Sigh, sigh]*."

*   *   *   *   *

Here's a typical dialog between a martyr and her self-righteous spouse. Try not to laugh too loud.

Wife: "I've got a terrible headache."

Husband: "Why don't you take some Tylenol?"

Wife: "I don't like to take medicine."

Husband: "All right then, shut up and enjoy your pain."

These lines are funny because they sound so familiar. They are exactly like conversations most of us have had with our own spouses or arguments we've heard our parents repeat over and over! There's really nothing new under the sun.

The language of "love"

Martyrs unwittingly use passive-aggressive language in order to dramatize their role as the underdog. Their choice of words is snide, self-victimizing. Their demeanor is angry and whining at the same time.

"I'm not allowed to do anything."

"I'm told by my wife that I'm a good-for-nothing so-and-so."

"I'm blamed for everything."

By using the passive rather than the active tense, the speaker positions himself as the victim: "This is being done *to* me. I'm totally innocent." Some martyrs even avoid using their partner's name when complaining about him or her through gritted teeth. Or they say the person's name as if it were a dirty word.

Dosing oneself to death

Many couples seem to be addicted to the power struggle itself. They literally fight to the death. This addiction can be as powerful as a cocaine addiction. From a biochemical standpoint, "winning" a battle creates a cocainelike high. Remember the movie *The War of the Roses*? That's a great illustration of this point.

I understand that cocaine is the only drug that laboratory animals will knowingly dose themselves to death on. I've seen martyrs who are so bent on winning an argument that they are willing to fight to the death of the relationship. Perhaps country music singer Kenny Chesney was describing double-martyr marriages when he sang, "You win. I win. *We* lose."[2]

In some double-martyr marriages, one or both partners are intellectually aware of the fact that they're risking their relationship, yet they persist in fighting with no apparent regard for anything holy or reasonable. They don't care how much they hurt themselves. And they show little concern for anyone who might be affected by their constant wrangling, such as innocent children. They attack each other's faults and defend their own rightness with a vengeance that is relationally suicidal. Like the drug addict, once they start using, they can't quit.

Some misery addicts smile sweetly and modulate their voices, but when the opportunity arises, they slip the knife between their partners' ribs. All that matters to them is winning. Gregory Lester describes this aptly in his book *Shrunken Heads*. Referring to the atmosphere in his childhood home, he says, "The problem was that while everyone acted like, talked like, and insisted that everything was fine, just *fine*, everyone felt bad—often very bad—essentially all the time. . . . Oh, and let us not forget the icicles hanging from the relationship between my parents as they poked and prodded each other with those ten foot poles."[3]

This is the ultimate example of powerlessness. Locked in mortal combat, such couples seem to relish being miserable and making sure that their partner is miserable too. They would rather torment each other than change. They wouldn't *think* of getting a divorce, because they enjoy torturing and being tortured too much. Some continue this pattern for a lifetime. Just before their fiftieth anniversary, they begin to wonder why they've wasted so many years.

The ultimate sacrifice—not!

The ultimate sacrifice two martyrs can make—not unlike being burned at the stake—is that of staying together for the sake of the children. They don't realize that their children will blame *themselves* for their parents' unhappiness. Meanwhile, the parents are using the kids as an excuse to do what they already want to do: punish each other eternally.

They don't seem to realize that they're not doing their children any favors by staying together and being miserable. If they *really* cared about the kids, they'd get help, grow up, and learn how to get along. Granted, this is easier said than done, but it's possible. Misery addicts who are willing to go to any lengths to arrest their addictive behavior *can* recover! From the psychological, moral, and social standpoints, this is the best option. However, if a couple cannot or will not do what's necessary to grow up and get happy, then divorce may be a better alternative than catching the children in the crossfire of an endless "covert war."

Research suggests that the children of divorced parents and the children of parents who remain unhappily glued together have the same kinds of self-esteem problems in later life. Why? The children of couples who stay together in spite of their misery are caught in the crossfire. I've yet to meet the first adult or child reared in this kind of hostile environment who appreciated their parents' noble sacrifice.

Mind you, I'm not making a case for divorce. I'm making a case for growing up and getting healthy, no matter what it takes! To accomplish this, parents may have to reach out for professional help to arrest their addictions and codependencies. It *can* be done—if both are willing to engage in individual therapy, twelve-step groups, and couples work with a qualified professional.

In some cases, it is virtually impossible to address the problems in the relationship directly until each partner has done a lot of work on his or her personal growth in therapy and twelve-step programs. People are generally not qualified to do couples work until they have addressed their own issues of immaturity in individual counseling. Once they have done this, they have the necessary resources to benefit from couples counseling.

Getting professional help requires an investment of time and money. It's not comfortable or convenient. But if you think you can't afford the time or money needed for therapy, you may want to consider the alternative. Divorce is more costly. *You are worth whatever it costs to get help, and your children are worth it too!* Please don't sell yourself and your offspring short! Excuse me for getting a little preachy here. I have rather strong convictions on this subject for personal, historical reasons.

I'll conclude with this testimony: Having worked with more than four thousand alcoholics, workaholics, and other addicts and their families in the treatment setting for the last thirty-three years, I know hundreds of couples whose marriages are thriving today because they had the courage to go to whatever lengths were necessary to grow themselves up as individuals and learn how to have happy, functional relationships. I would count my own marriage as one of them.

Hope for Today

A relationship can be only as healthy as both partners are willing and able to make it. When both are committed to going to whatever lengths are necessary to change their negative habits of thinking, believing, and behaving into positive, mature social skills, everyone wins. Wishful thinking isn't enough. Sometimes, even earnest prayer is insufficient. Faith without work—putting effort into a process of healing—won't get the job done. Faith *and* work will.

Self-Study

1. Did your parents argue (power struggle) a lot? Did they model healthy resolution of their differences? Or did they fight fruitlessly?

2. Did you develop a sense of foreboding when they were at odds with each other? Were you afraid that one of them would leave and never come back? And if one *did* leave, did you blame yourself?

3. If alcoholism or any other addiction was present in your home, please consider finding an Adult Children of Alcoholics (ACoA) meeting where you can share your feelings with others who have a similar background. See Appendix G for details.

---

1. Earnie Larsen, *Stage II Recovery* (New York: HarperOne, 1987).

2. Kenny Chesney, "You Win, I Win, We Lose," *I Will Stand* (BNA Entertainment, 1997). Emphasis added.

3. Gregory Lester, *Shrunken Heads: The Insane, the Profane, and the Profound on the Road to Becoming a Psychologist* (Houston, Tex.: Ashcroft Press, 2005), 3.

Martyring by Caregiving

A pessimist is one who, when he has the choice of two evils, chooses both.
— Oscar Wilde

Most martyrs reach the point where they are no longer victims. They're *volunteers.* Convinced that they are responsible for everyone's health and happiness (everyone's but their own, that is), they base their worth on their ability to sacrifice themselves with little or no regard for their own health and safety.

I've met many lovely people who rely on the caretaker persona for meaning, identity, and value. Frankly, I'm one of them. Prior to recovery, I was emotionally dependent on the shot of self-esteem I got from rescuing and repairing people. I needed to be needed. I wouldn't have considered abstaining from ministering to others, even if my life or the welfare of my loved ones had depended on it (and it often did)!

Sixteen-year-old Kelly described a conversation between herself and her mother that is a painful reminder to me: "My mom thinks she's Mother Theresa. She runs all over the place helping people, giving them Bible studies, buying them clothes, furniture, whatever. She's never home. Yesterday, I told her I wished she would spend less time helping others and more time hanging out with Dad and me. I couldn't believe what she said, 'How can I do any less when Jesus gave His *life* for me?'

How could I argue with that? Ten minutes later she left the house to go on another of God's errands."

This well-meaning woman's determination to perform her Christian duty would have been OK if she could have sacrificed herself without sacrificing her family. But that was impossible. She made people into projects. And once she undertook a project, she couldn't let it go. She was driven to do more and more. Sounds like a bona fide addiction, doesn't it? In the face of obvious negative consequences, she continued her self-destructive behavior. The belief that fueled her striving was that she was responsible—not just for her neighbors' *happiness*—but for their *salvation* as well. She isn't the first person to act on a biblical mandate in an extreme manner rather than taking a balanced, moderate approach.

Incidentally, her attempts to rescue and repair people are sometimes invasive and unwelcome. Her subjects take offense at her dogged attempts to "save" them. More prospective church members are driven *from* God and church than are drawn *to* God and church by such behavior, but caregivers who are intent on saving someone are oblivious to this fact. Take note: in our efforts to do our "Christian duty," we need to respect people's personal boundaries.

Mixed motives

Caretakers are at risk for becoming Class *A* champion martyrs. Some are thoroughbred whiners too. They rarely perform a service for God, church, or country without expecting a reward—eternal or otherwise. And they are prone to complain if their sacrifices go unnoticed or unappreciated. As Dr. Paul Tournier puts it in *A Place for You:* "A certain more-or-less conscious egoism always lurks behind the pleasure one derives from devoting oneself to others."[1] In other words, what appears to be self*less*ness can be self*fish*ness if we do it to make ourselves feel good.

Does this mean that everyone who does something nice for another person is being selfish? Not at all. It simply means that when we have the urge to be helpful, we need to examine our motives. If we're doing something for someone that they *should* do for themselves or something they haven't asked us to do or something that has a negative impact on us or our families, we need to restrain ourselves.

The appropriate alternative is to mind our own business and pray for them instead of trying to rescue them. But pray in your closet. Don't announce it from the pulpit or publish it in the local newspaper. Many martyrs would take it as an insult if you told them you were praying for them, especially if you said it in public.

Caregiving behaviors

World-class caregivers

- try to make themselves indispensable to others;
- anticipate other people's needs and fulfill them;
- do things for people that those individuals *should* do for themselves;
- give disrespectfully, that is, without consulting the recipient's preferences;
- give without permission—foist unsolicited advice or assistance on people;
- give to get, whether the payoff is appreciation, gratification, or a shot of self-esteem;
- give to gain control, the rationale being, "After all I've done for you, I have the right to tell you what to do";
- give generously but complain afterward, which is a subtle form of bragging.

When his seven-year marriage ended, Kevin, a nurse in his late thirties, began to use caregiving as a way to occupy lonely hours and fulfill his need to be needed. Because he was extremely versatile, he volunteered to help friends and former patients in every way he could. He remodeled their houses, repaired their cars, and fixed their broken appliances. He was more popular than the Maytag repairman, because he never charged his "customers" a penny!

Kevin was a professional caregiver by trade, but other forms of caregiving became his avocation. His need for attention and approval drove him to work harder and harder. He wasn't concerned about making money. Pleasing people was payment enough.

His schedule became increasingly hectic. He grew weary from overwork and lack of sleep. In order to keep up the pace, Kevin increased his caffeine intake. When he injured himself while overhauling his cousin's car engine, he added narcotic painkillers to his regimen. It was downhill from there. He popped pills on a regular basis to avoid the pain and exhaustion brought on by his excessive behavior. Eventually, he became a full-blown addict, which nearly cost him his career and his life.

The consequences of Matthew's caretaking were different than Kevin's. Husband and father of five, Matt was a leader in his church and community. When his pastor encouraged the congregation to seek out needy souls and win them to the Lord by providing for their material needs and then inviting them to church (in secular settings, this is known as the bait-and-switch technique), Matt began looking for someone who needed help.

He met an ideal candidate—Tony, a troubled teenager who was in desperate need of a father figure. When Matt's wife, Maria, learned that the troubled teenager was the same age as their oldest daughter, she tactfully cautioned Matt about the risks of befriending him. In spite of her warnings, Matt persisted. He even invited the young man to live in their home. Then he proceeded to let him get away with things he didn't allow his own children to do.

The children were confused by the double standard. Their father was compromising the values and principles he had instilled in them. Their mother begged Matt to turn his charge over to the care of professionals who were more qualified to help him, but Matt could not bring himself to do so, even in the interest of protecting his kids.

The fact that he couldn't stop caretaking the boy, even though he recognized the risks to his own children, speaks volumes about the addictive nature of Matt's caretaking. He made rescuing and repairing Tony his highest priority. He did so to the detriment of himself and his family, and he continued to do so in the face of adverse consequences. This is a hallmark of addiction. Eventually, his daughter ran away with the boy and became involved with drugs.

Matt is not alone in his misplaced zeal. My husband and I have martyred ourselves similarly and, in so doing, put the welfare of our children at risk. One of our adult sons told us when he was eighteen that our obsession with helping troubled people led him to believe that he had to be troubled in order to get our attention! That was a wakeup call for us. But we didn't do anything about it. We didn't heed the warning until years later.

The consequences of "professional" martyring

As a counselor, I've seen many children of ministers and missionaries who have been sacrificed for causes to which their parents were truly dedicated. While the sincerity of the parents is unquestionable, there's no way they could have foreseen—or foresworn—the impact of their self-sacrificial behavior on the lives of their children. These young people are at risk for a multitude of ills: low self-esteem, crippling self-doubt, social ineptitude, marital problems, addiction, codependence, clinical depression, and anxiety disorders. The message they absorbed in childhood was, "You matter, but just not as much as . . ."

There's a fine line between setting an altruistic example to one's children and being a compulsive caregiver. We parents don't always recognize the risk we're taking. But I wish I had a dollar for every pastor or pastor's wife, missionary or missionary's wife, church administrator or spouse of a church administrator, who has said to me, "I wish I had known how my decisions were going to affect my children. Why didn't someone tell me?"

I echo their frustration. The fact that we want to sacrifice our lives for God or country doesn't give us the right to martyr our innocent offspring. I'm aware of many parents who have insisted on remaining in dangerous mission outposts in countries torn by civil strife, thus exposing their children to horrendous violence. There was a time when I myself would have considered this appropriate. No longer. I have seen the long-range consequences in the lives of too many adult children of altruistic parents.

I salute those dedicated humanitarians who have given their lives in devoted service to the physically and spiritually starved peoples of the earth. I pray that their children have not had to suffer unduly. I identify with the struggle to balance the needs of family with the demands of Christian ministry and other causes. I would never want to heap guilt on anyone whose children suffered negative consequences when they were doing their best to serve humankind. If we don't forgive ourselves for the mistakes we made in the times of our ignorance, we will be martyring ourselves once more. We can take responsibility by making ourselves accountable for the impact of our behavior on our children so they won't have to bear the emotional and spiritual burden of shame and self-blame alone.

During the recent genocide in Rwanda, a missionary couple who had just returned to the United States was interviewed on a local television show. Sitting with their toddlers in front of the cameras, they described the atrocities they had witnessed. Then they stated that they were urging their mission board to send them back to Rwanda as quickly as possible. They could hardly wait to return.

As I listened to their testimony, I felt ill, nauseous. Why? Because I was counseling a woman at that very time who was depressed and suicidal as a result of a similar childhood experience. When she was three, *her* missionary parents had insisted on staying in a country torn by civil strife in order to protect mission property. After her unexplainable "nervous breakdown" thirty years later, she recalled seeing guns being held to her parents' heads by guerillas, body parts scattered in the streets, and truckloads of corpses passing by the mission compound years before.

She recalled how she and her family barricaded themselves in the living room of their home to avoid stray bullets. They built a cave out of mattresses and stayed inside for days. Once, when gunfire erupted while she was playing in the courtyard of the mission compound, she and her father leaped into a foxhole that had been dug for just such an occasion. When they climbed out after the fighting ended, they found one of her sandals in the yard. It had been blown to bits while she was crouching in the foxhole wearing the matching shoe.

Her parents always assured her that God would protect them, as well He did. But their reassurance didn't relieve her fears or keep her from being traumatized. In adulthood, she succumbed to post-traumatic stress disorder and nearly lost her life. Later, she expressed her feelings in a letter she wrote as part of her therapy but didn't mail:

> Mom and Dad,
> I was terrified, and you didn't comfort me. I was angry, and you said to smile. I was hungry, and you grabbed food from my hands. You told me not to give in to appetite. I was in danger,

and you said God would protect us; lonely, and you said, "Don't bother me; I have to go to work." I was naked and bleeding from being molested by a houseboy, and you said Jesus would forgive *me*. I was sick, and I had to go to the doctor alone; poor, and you took my money to give to the less fortunate. You made me sleep on the floor. I was tired and hot, and you said, "Dry up!" I was mistaken, and you beat me. I was your child, and you never knew me. And when I said I wanted to die, you shouted, *Why?*

Another missionary's daughter reported that the mission compound where she and her family were stationed was broken into frequently by thieves, yet her father left his wife and children alone for weeks at a time while he was ministering to the needs of the nationals. She too was assured that God would send His angels to protect them, but she lived in abject terror.

Chronic fear creates elevated cortisol and adrenaline levels, which has serious medical consequences. Children who live in a state of unrelenting stress are at risk for any number of social and emotional problems in later life, some of which are partially attributable to the early effects of trauma on their brain chemistry. Some end up paying for their parents' martyring behavior with their own lives. Society disdains alcoholics who sacrifice their families for the sake of booze. Is this any different? If well-meaning, self-sacrificial parents knew the potential consequences of their decisions, perhaps they would behave differently. I like to think that I would have been less inclined to martyr myself and my family if I had known then what I know now, but I'm not certain. I don't know if I *could* have done any differently, because I am the granddaughter of a workaholic missionary, and I was just obeying the rules.

Killing ourselves and others with kindness

Children reared in alcoholic or otherwise addictive environments are schooled to take responsibility for the physical and emotional well-being of others. They cope with difficult circumstances by caretaking people when they are young, leaving themselves at risk for compulsive caretaking and undue self-sacrifice in adulthood. They may be genuinely kind and willing to do almost anything to make others happy. But eventually, they begin to rely on caretaking for self-esteem and value. Fearful of being abandoned, they try to make themselves indispensable by seeking out needy people to help. Some literally collect "cripples."

Ministers, missionaries, public servants, social workers, medical practitioners, and other helping professionals are inclined to this behavior because so many of them come from alcoholic family backgrounds. Experts estimate that more than 80 percent of all nurses, doctors, pastors, and counselors are adult children of alcoholic or dysfunctional families, which means that they are codependent.[2] Undue self-sacrifice is second nature to them. They compromise their physical and mental health and neglect their families in order to rescue and repair others.

In some cases, they harm the ones they are trying to help as much or more than they benefit them. In the process, they put themselves on the fast track to burnout. This is a serious matter. Individuals who intend to go into helping professions need to inoculate themselves against compulsive caretaking by treating their own wounds before they take up their duties as professional caretakers. They need to therapeutically address the damage done to them in childhood before beginning their careers.

Childhood and adolescent development are disrupted by addiction or abuse. Children growing up in these circumstances are not adequately nurtured, and children who don't receive adequate nurturing don't grow up. They remain socially and emotionally immature. If they fail to deal with their issues of immaturity before beginning their careers as helping professionals, sooner or later they will shortchange themselves and their clients, patients, or parishioners.

Not only do helping professionals need to be inoculated prior to pursuing their careers, they need booster shots throughout. They must enlist the help of other professionals—therapists, supervisors, twelve-step support groups, and sponsors indefinitely in order to protect themselves, their families, and their clients from harm.

This excerpt from a letter written by a missionary underscores the vulnerability of professional caregivers:

I have always been the "helper/rescuer" type of person. Maybe that's why my husband and I accepted this call to mission service. . . . Now *we* need help. My husband is suffering with his second encounter with burnout, and I am severely depressed.

How do we reconcile the problem of "loving too much" with all the things we've been taught about service? Somehow, I think missionaries in general need help. They have so many relationship problems. Living on a mission compound has to be the most abnormal thing! We have observed burnout, marital problems, and relationship problems between missionaries and the nationals. They tend to keep us in a "helper" role because they have incredible needs—illness, poverty, death, etc. We don't work together as coworkers (equals), and it's not healthy.

Healthy caring versus unhealthy caregiving

How does one distinguish between healthy caring and unhealthy caregiving on a practical level? There are distinct differences. Healthy caring is being genuinely concerned about the needs of others, while at the same time letting them take responsibility for themselves and their problems. We must not rush to rescue them. We don't feel compelled to fix them. By contrast, compulsive caregivers cannot emotionally detach themselves from anyone who is suffering. They can't stand to see people in pain; they *have* to rescue them.

Healthy *caring* is showing respectful concern for another person by sharing one's personal experience, strength, and hope without invading his or her boundaries, giving only when asked, and helping without expectation of reward. Unhealthy *caregiving* is doing things for another person that he should do for himself, trying to solve his problems, minding his business, violating his boundaries in order to rescue or fix him, managing his life, monitoring his conscience. Such behaviors keep the recipient sick and render him or her infantile. As Melody Beattie says, "Caregiving looks like a much friendlier act than it is. It requires incompetency on the part of the person being taken care of."[3]

In order to demonstrate healthy caring, caregivers need to let go of loved ones and their problems and allow them to grow up. They need to stand back and let them learn how to deal with their own difficulties and enjoy the self-respect that comes from doing so.

When Joclyn's son was thirty, she was still balancing his checkbook, paying his bills, and giving *her* credit references as if they were his to his creditors. She felt compelled to help him because he was an out-of-control addict. In reality, by taking over his responsibilities and protecting him from the consequences of his irresponsibility, she was helping him stay sick—perpetuating his illness and his immaturity. This is a classic example of enabling.

It's OK to say No to friends or family members in order to take care of one's own needs. Crystal, a small business owner, planned to spend the afternoon at home catching up on her mail. Five minutes after she arrived and settled down in her favorite rocker with a cup of tea and a stack of mail, her mother-in-law called and asked Crystal to drive her to the hairdresser. She couldn't refuse, but she resented the inconvenience. A good rule of thumb: if you can't do something without resentment, don't do it! Or change your attitude before you do it.

Nanette had a magnetic personality. So many people came to her with their problems that her friends started calling her "Nan Landers." When anyone requested her help, she invariably dropped whatever she was doing and rushed to their aid. Her parents had modeled this kind of behavior when she was young. Once, her pastor father canceled a highly anticipated family event in order to attend an emergency church board meeting. Years later, while Nanette was grieving her losses in therapy, she insisted—through her tears—that he had done the right thing.

Healthy caretakers are happy, content, serene, unhurried. *Compulsive* caretakers are stressed, weary, worn out, resentful. Healthy caregivers are able to accept help as well as give it. Compulsive caretakers nurture others but will not accept nurturing in return. They're assertive when attacking a social injustice or acting on behalf of others, but they can't be assertive when it comes to asking for what *they* want or need. They would rather withdraw or pout than ask.

Helping that helps versus helping that doesn't help

In order to help others in a healthy manner, we should wait for them to ask for our assistance. Imposing unsolicited advice or assistance is intrusive. It's OK to fix *things*—but not people. Compulsive caretakers rush in where angels fear to tread. Vicky is a classic example. She can't stand to see her grown daughter's apartment in a mess. Every time she visits, she goes on a cleaning spree that leaves her exhausted. Afterward, she complains bitterly to her husband. Her daughter is highly offended by her mother's actions. Giving generously but bragging or complaining afterward is a symptom of unhealthy caregiving.

Caregivers need to learn to receive as readily as they give. Overexhausting themselves in the service of others not only compromises their physical immune system, but it blows away their emotional safety net as well. Many clergy, church administrators, counselors, politicians, and physicians ruin their lives by behaving badly when their emotional safety net has been compromised. This could be avoided if they would take better care of themselves.

One final note to anyone who is in the habit of putting other people's needs before their own or hurting themselves to help others: if you have tried to control or curtail your compulsive caregiving, if you have done your best to practice healthy self-care and found that you cannot do it consistently, please consider treating the problem as an addiction and getting professional help.

Hope for Today

Regret and remorse are the hallmarks of misery addiction. Wallowing in remorse feeds my misery and turns me into very unpleasant company. If I don't want to drive the people I love out of my life, I need to change. Miserable moms are no fun. Freedom from guilt and maudlin self-reflection comes with working the Twelve Steps. I will engage in this process with my sponsor's help so that I don't have to impose my guilt and shame on the people who have already been hurt enough by my addiction and codependence. My significant others are willing to forgive. I don't have to pay penance. Wallowing in guilt will serve no purpose except to maintain my misery.

Self-Study

1. When you were young, did you find it necessary to take care of or comfort anyone close to you? How did you protect them or try to take away their pain?
2. How were you rewarded for your effort?
3. Did being kind and helpful become part of your persona?
4. Have you ever taken caretaking to the extreme and ended up hurting yourself or harming someone else?
5. Make a list of the negative consequences of your excessive caretaking. Turn to a source of wisdom and strength outside yourself, God, as you understand God, or a good friend, and express your feelings of pain and remorse.

---

1. Paul Tournier, *A Place for You* (New York: Harper & Row, 1968), 109.

2. Sharon Wegscheider-Cruse quoted in Ann Wilson Schaef, *When Society Becomes an Addict* (New York: Harper & Row, 1987), 30.

3. Melody Beattie, *Codependent No More,* 79.

The Fine Art of Overdoing Everything

There can't be a crisis next week. My schedule is already full.
— Henry Kissinger

In chapter 8, we looked at the mess martyring and caretaking create when you mix them together. Martyring blends handily with several other addictions as well: workaholism, perfectionism, compulsive controlling, and religious addiction or legalism.

Each of these combination plates offers a unique set of problems. But before we address the characteristics and consequences of the various combinations, we need to study another basic question: How does one determine whether a given lifestyle practice is normal or addictive? Even negativity can be normal if it is balanced with an adequate amount of positivity, or so says Dr. Barbara Fredrickson, psychology professor at the University of Michigan. The optimal ratio of positive to negative affect is approximately three to one.[1]

Most clean addictions fall within gray areas. They involve actions like eating, working, or worshiping—activities that are appropriate and necessary. We can't live without working, performing our duties reasonably well, making plans, and engaging in spiritual pursuits. Differentiating between normal and addictive behavior is difficult in these areas. How do we know when a normal relationship with something or someone has become an unhealthy dependence? In the previous chapter we discussed the difference between healthy caring and unhealthy caregiving. Here are some other concerns: How do we distinguish between working to live and living to work? Is there a difference between healthy achievement and neurotic perfectionism? How do we differentiate between compulsive controlling and just being responsible? And what's the difference between healthy spirituality and obsessive religiosity?

All-purpose addicts

Some people are so versatile that they can turn almost anything into an addiction. This includes activities like eating, not eating, sleeping, not sleeping, being sexually promiscuous, being sexually anorexic, overexercising, being a couch potato, shopping compulsively, hoarding money, gambling, fantasizing, playing video games, surfing the Internet, decorating, gardening, scrapbooking, knitting, waxing floors, talking, joking, watching TV, and writing books.

While conservative religious people are somewhat less likely than others to abuse drugs and alcohol, they are *more* likely to abuse food, work, religion, caregiving, control, and gossip. People can harm themselves in a million ways, many of which seem quite harmless. *The nature of a given substance or activity does not determine its addictive potential.* Addiction is defined—not by *what* we do or how much we do it—but by *why* we do it and the consequences that follow.

Martyring by overworking

As surely as misery addicts are attracted to abusive partners, they are drawn to institutions that engage in the kinds of behavior—control, manipulation, double standards, triangulation, and secret keeping—that are typical of dysfunctional families. Many administrators of such institutions are actively addicted, usually to work. Often, a majority of the employees are adult survivors of addiction or abuse and are thus very codependent. In some cases, the agency demands an addictive devotion to its mission.[2]

I once heard a church leader boasting about the fact that people who drove past the church offices at any hour of the day or night would see lights on and employees hard at work. I don't believe he realized the implications of his statement. Burning the candle at both ends leads to burnout. Leaders who overwork risk their physical, emotional, and spiritual health and fail to model moderation and balance to their constituency. Yet executives, politicians, medical professionals, businessmen, and clergy live this way all the time. Generations of church members have come to expect it of their pastors.

Workaholics are drug addicts who are hooked on endogenous chemicals, drugs produced in their own bodies. Unlike street drugs that must be procured illegally, the workaholic's drug of choice is readily available and doesn't cost a penny. Although he doesn't go to dangerous neighborhoods or spend hard-earned cash to buy it, the workaholic pays a high price in terms of his or her physical health and social and emotional well-being. Stress-related illness is the inevitable result: heart attacks, strokes, and hypertension. This is martyring to the max.

The first time someone accused me of being a workaholic, I took it as an insult and responded defensively, "I'm not a workaholic. I *love* my work." Right. Cocaine addicts love their cocaine too! The fact that I enjoyed my work didn't negate the fact that I was getting high on adrenaline. It actually confirmed it.

While workaholism is an officially approved addiction in many social settings, it is no less unwise or immoral than alcoholism when viewed from the standpoint of the biblical mandate to treat our bodies as God's temple. Religiously motivated workaholics would do well to face this unpleasant reality.

Working to live versus living to work

I considered asking someone else to write this part, because I'm not sure I have resolved this issue completely in my own life. The fact is that I am and always will be a workaholic—something I cannot afford to forget. Actually, that may be my best qualification for writing on the subject! Alcoholics Anonymous literature suggests that the most any recovering alcoholic can hope for is a daily reprieve from his symptoms contingent on the maintenance of a spiritual program. I am not ashamed to say that one day at a time and by the grace of God, I am a recovering caretaker, controller, workaholic, and martyr.

Prior to recovery, I didn't realize that normal people don't start thinking about work the minute they wake up in the morning. They don't hook themselves up to a computer and download a to-do list for themselves and everyone around them (spouse, children, employees) before breakfast. Normal people exist apart from work. They don't define themselves by their professional role. They don't accept more responsibility than they can handle. They don't obsess about work when they're not at work. They don't take work with them on holidays. They don't have to finish a project before they can stop or take a break. They can put tasks on hold. They take time to go to the bathroom. They go for walks and smell the flowers. Even if they *could* get a task done today, they can put it off until tomorrow without feeling guilty. They work to live. They don't live to work.

I appreciate a simple motto I learned at Workaholics Anonymous: "I am enough. I have enough. I do enough." Amen.

Putting perfectionism in perspective

Doing the right thing and *believing* the right things have always been important to me. As a small child, I was painfully conscientious. In elementary school, I wasted reams of paper recopying my math assignments over and over until the margins were straight and the columns of numbers perfectly aligned. In adolescence, I placed unrealistic demands on myself, graduating from high school at sixteen and college at nineteen. For the next twenty years, my perfectionism drove me to the point that it affected my mental health and hurt the people closest to me.

Perfectionism is about needing to be right. Technically, there's nothing wrong with being right but being *obsessed* with being right *is* questionable. It's not healthy to make being right and righteous our sole source of meaning, identity, and value. When we measure our own worth and judge the worth of our peers by the quality of our or their performance, perfectionism takes on an offensive quality at best, an addictive quality at worst.

According to Al-Anon literature, the compulsive drive for perfection can be a neurotic symptom as difficult to deal with as the alcoholic's compulsion to drink.[3] I can testify to that fact. Perfectionism isn't attractive. It doesn't draw people to us; it drives them away. People run from perfectionists because they feel so defective in their presence. And they're irritated by the perfectionist's pickiness and the subtle arrogance of perfectionism in general.

In a charming book entitled *The Art of Imperfection,* Veronique Vienne says, "Our innate idiosyncrasies are actually more endearing to others than our most glorious personal achievements. History is full of incompetent people who were beloved, blunderers with winsome personality traits, and inept folks who delighted their entourages with their unassuming presences. Their secret? To accept their flaws with the same grace and humility as their best qualities."[4]

There's no penalty for not being able to walk on water, she adds. One can make quite an impression by ordering a second serving of dessert on a date or setting the stove on fire while cooking a fancy meal. Notice this touch of realism: "You're a smart lawyer, but your kids adore you because you make scary faces. You've just been elected president of the board, but your best friend says, 'You fooled them, didn't you?' "[5]

Vienne offers an appealing description of an imperfect world, a society in which people don't spend an inordinate amount of time and energy fuming against their fate whenever they make a mistake. They can "bump into furniture, miss deadlines, get lost on the way to the airport, forget to return phone calls, and show up at parties a day early without getting unduly annoyed with themselves."[6] Although most people believe the adage "to err is human," many consider themselves the exception to the rule. "What's good enough for you isn't good enough for me. Make a mistake? Not on my watch!"[7] They cling to this attitude, even though it doesn't bring them peace and serenity. Nor does it add to their popularity.

Newsflash: There is a God, and I am not Him (Her, It). In the final analysis, no one's happiness or salvation depends upon my exemplary behavior. People enjoy hanging out with human beings like themselves, not with paragons of pathological perfectionism. Our humanness is what qualifies us to be useful to others—not our flawlessness.

This is not to say that the pursuit of excellence is bad or that embracing high moral values is wrong. But if we want to have a winsome faith, a viable witness, we need to step down from our pedestals! Says Vienne, "Whenever in a moral quandary, do the right thing. But don't consider that having principles makes you special, superior, or heroic. If, on the other hand, you fail to be as ethical as you think you should have been, don't act surprised."[8]

How does perfectionism interface with misery addiction? Being unable to accept their fallibility, perfectionists place themselves under enormous pressure. They are obsessed with their performance. Getting an A isn't enough—they have to get the top A. They pursue excellence as if their lives depended on it—and sometimes it does. I've known many perfectionists, myself included, whose first thoughts of suicide (in my case, at the age of thirteen) came on the heels of a less-than-perfect performance.

How to know if you're a perfectionist

By way of self-assessment, notice how you react to failure. Do you feel worthless when you don't perform perfectly? Does your mood take a nosedive? Do you deny your faults and blame others in order to maintain your illusion of perfection? Do you use flawless behavior to protect your damaged ego? If so, you may be a perfectionist. Be not dismayed. You can change.

The pursuit of imperfection

Some perfectionists, especially those who practice their perfectionism in the context of religion, need to start by assessing their theology and developing a more accurate understanding of God's character. Hopefully, they will discover that God's love and approval don't fluctuate on the basis of their performance.

Here are a few suggestions for abstinence from perfectionism:

- Stop managing your image. Drop the phony façade and accept the fact that you are perfectly imperfect.
- Celebrate progress—not perfection.
- Occasionally, do the minimum, put less than the usual amount of effort into achieving a goal.
- Wear mismatched or stained clothing without apologizing or explaining.
- Quell the internal critic—cut yourself and others a whole lot of slack.
- Focus on something pure, good, lovely in yourself or someone else.
- Drop the take-charge persona—let someone else be in charge.
- Ask for and accept help frequently.
- If at first you don't succeed, *don't* try again.
- Say "I don't know," "I'm not sure," or "I'd rather not" several times a day.

- Pray for humility.
- Laugh at yourself when you trip and fall and be sure to tell your friends about it.
- And remember, don't act surprised when you make a mistake!

Taking charge of self versus controlling others

The more we feel compelled to manage and control people and circumstances, the more we have to sacrifice ourselves, ignore our own needs, or risk our health and safety, to accomplish our mission. You and I are responsible for our own lives, but it is not our job to manage other people's lives. Consider this: the minute I start trying to control your behavior, I'm operating on the premise that I know what's best for you or that I have a corner on knowledge of God's will.

Even if I *were* privy to knowledge of God's will for your life, I wouldn't know the appropriate *timing* or the route (including detours) that you might need to take along the way. I don't know what's best for you, and if I try to assume control of what you do, say, think, feel, or believe, I'm playing God—a role which I'm not at all qualified for.

How do martyrs manipulate and control? By giving orders, directly or indirectly, making plans without consulting those affected, demanding instead of asking, assuming the right to manage people's lives, and refusing to take No for an answer. "Sister Brown, if you don't accept the job of Vacation Bible School director this year, we probably won't be able to have a Vacation Bible School." Shaming someone for saying No isn't OK.

Manipulators hint instead of asking directly; they argue, blame, shame, and employ charm to get their way, play politics, engage in verbal or physical abuse, threaten others subtly, and behave passive-aggressively when all else fails.

Unhealthy control: managing others

Negative or unhealthy control is invading another person's boundaries, minding his or her business, assuming the right to manage his or her life—health, language, manners, beliefs, standards—trying to force outcomes, interpreting God's will for him or her, and trying to be his or her conscience or Higher Power.

How does controlling link up with misery addiction? Compulsive controllers are happy (satisfied) only when they can get everyone else to act right. They believe there's only one right way to do something, and they're the only one who knows what it is. In social situations, controllers often assume the self-appointed role of "cruise director." They take on leadership responsibilities that haven't been assigned to them and exhaust themselves trying to arrange people and circumstances to their liking. When people don't yield to their wishes, they are miserable and miserable to be around. Need I say more?

Compulsive controllers can create a lot of havoc in the workplace, in churches, and on boards and committees. If things don't go their way, everybody pays. I have seen bitterness and resentment develop in churches and other social groups around minor differences of opinion that recycled themselves for two or more generations, maintaining a spirit of dissension long after the details of the initial squabble were forgotten. I believe this is a symptom of undiagnosed, untreated addiction to caretaking and control.

Healthy controlling: taking charge of self

Is it possible to control in a healthy way? Indeed, it is. Positive or healthy control is *self*-control—taking charge of your life and making yourself responsible for your own well-being and that of your minor children.

One of the biggest challenges of our adult lives is breaking the habit of controlling and caretaking our children when they are grown. Because I consider Al-Anon to be kindergarten for healthy detachment, I recommend it to all parents who are trying to withdraw from managing their children's lives, even if the children have never picked up a drink or drug.

Healthy spirituality versus addictive religiosity (legalism)

The interaction between religious addiction and martyring is somewhat natural. In certain circumstances, sacrificing one's life for the Lord or for a good cause *is* appropriate and necessary, but only when one is *called spiritually* to do so—not when one is *driven by addiction and codependence*. Recognizing the fine line between these two extremes requires tremendous self-awareness and spiritual maturity.

Many scriptural heroes were called to martyrdom—John the Baptist, the apostle Paul, Stephen, etc. Numerous pioneers of successful religious movements, Martin Luther, James and Ellen White, Joseph Smith, Joseph Bates, and others, made enormous sacrifices for the sake of others. Many national heroes have taken huge risks and made incredible sacrifices for causes they believed in, Mother Teresa, Martin Luther King Jr., and Nelson Mandela, to name a few.

Healthy self-sacrifice

People practicing healthy spirituality are free to make sane choices about self-sacrificial behavior and maintain balance and moderation in their religious disciplines, including giving. But those who are practicing religious addiction are likely to carry their self-sacrificial behavior to the extreme, often martyring themselves unnecessarily. Or they do the right thing for the wrong reasons: to earn their salvation, gain approval, or manage their image. Most overextend themselves. They work for the Lord with demonic frenzy and beat themselves and others up in their attempts to manage the universe.

Those who rationalize and justify these behaviors on the basis of God and church are twisting what is meant to be the most positive part of their lives and turning it into an instrument of self-abuse—something I know from personal experience. I don't think that's what God had in mind. Thankfully, the God of my understanding doesn't condemn people who wittingly or unwittingly do these things, anymore than He condemns any other addict.

Religious addiction is no better and no worse than chemical dependence. All addictions have consequences. Every addict needs and deserves forgiveness, mercy, and grace. Unfortunately, misery addicts have trouble accepting it, which is one of the most serious symptoms of their addiction. More on that later.

Hope for Today

God, help me to accept Your grace, bask in Your goodness, and remember that Your approval is not conditional. Help me not to condemn myself or anyone else for being human and thus imperfect. Help me to celebrate the mistakes I make as nothing more or less than opportunities to learn and grow. Above all, give me the gift of moderation and balance. And help me not to act shocked or to be discouraged when I mess up.

Self-Study

1. Was there a workaholic or perfectionist in your family of origin? How did that person rationalize his or her behavior? Did you buy into his or her philosophy?
2. From the perspective of the wounded part of yourself, write a letter expressing the sadness and loneliness you felt when your significant other was physically or emotionally unavailable to you.
3. In your adult life, have you deprived yourself or your loved ones of the time and attention that you and they deserve because you are so busy being perfect? What has this cost you?
4. Allow yourself to grieve your losses. Find a photo of yourself as a youngster and read your letter to him or her. If music helps put you in touch with your feelings, play it during this exercise. (This suggestion is not only for women; men need to mourn their losses too.) Share your feelings with a trusted friend.

---

1. Z. Stambor, " 'Appropriate' Negativity Necessary for People to Prosper," *American Psychological Association Online*, http://www.apa.org/monitor/nov05/appropriate.html. (Accessed August 22, 2007.)

2. Anne Wilson Schaef and Diane Fassel, *The Addictive Organization* (San Francisco: Harper & Row, 1990), 118.

3. Al-Anon Family Group, *One Day at a Time in Al-Anon* (New York: Al-Anon World Services, 1958), 358.

4. Ibid.

5. Ibid.

6. Ibid.

7. Ibid.

8. Ibid.

CHAPTER 10

A Field Guide to Whining and Complaining

There are two days in the week on which I never worry:
one is yesterday, and the other is tomorrow.

— Robert Burdette

A martyr's needs are few: something to make her miserable, and someone to blame for her misery. In chapter 9, we looked at how misery addiction interfaces with certain clean addictions and how they exacerbate one another. But there is an even more dramatic synergy when the dually addicted person is hooked on a *dirty* substance or activity, such as drugs, alcohol, or sex, *plus* misery. These individuals have a ready-made rationale for getting high, a logical excuse for acting out. Their designated persecutor, usually a spouse or parent, provides them with a perfect alibi for drinking, drugging, having affairs, etc.

Everyday annoyances stimulate the adrenaline required to propel dually addicted martyrs into the various hells where they feel most comfortable and provide them with a "valid" reason for indulging in their favorite dirty addiction: "You'd drink too, if you had a wife like mine," they insist. "You'd overeat, overwork, or overcontrol too, if your husband was as cranky as mine." "You'd have affairs, gamble compulsively, or watch X-rated movies too, if your wife was as fat as mine or your husband was as boring as mine or your kids were as badly behaved as mine."

Most of the misery addict's complaints fall into one of four categories: physical maladies, financial woes, social problems, and past insults to the psyche. I used to think that these organ recitals (*oh,* my liver) were a phenomenon of old age, but now I know that young martyrs can complain about their sciatica right along with the best of us. Chronic complaining keeps the misery addict locked in inaction, which ensures that his problems will persist, thus providing him with plenty of fodder for further complaining.

What does the negaholic have to do to abstain from acting out? At what point can he or she interrupt the cycle? And, for goodness' sake, what is she or he trying to abstain from?

The challenge of distinguishing abstinence from "using"

Recovery begins with abstinence, and abstinence is a frustratingly vague concept for anyone suffering from clean addictions. Alcoholics abstain from drinking by putting the cork in the bottle and keeping it there. Drug addicts abstain by removing the needle from their arms or refusing to take the pill, smoke the joint, or snort the powder. But—*eek, screech, stop*—how do misery addicts abstain?

As we have seen, most clean addictions involve lifestyle behaviors that one can't totally stop doing and still survive—eating, working, exercising, relating to people, and so on. Abstinence is defined by moderation and balance rather than by refraining totally from the behavior. This poses a significant challenge. As Augustine put it, "Complete abstinence is easier than perfect moderation." So let's all heave a big sigh of sympathy for misery addicts, because it's so much harder for them to define and practice abstinence than it is for other addicts. *Awwww.*

Some twelve-step groups leave the definition of abstinence to the individual, whose own "enlightened self-interest" determines the when and how of it.[1] I'm not sure what *enlightened self-interest* means, but I interpret it as self-understanding—being aware of one's weaknesses, honest about what is likely to trigger cravings, and willing to avoid the toxic people, places, and things that set one up to behave addictively.

So let's examine the meaning of *using.* This will help us distinguish between abstinence and acting out. This ensuing material will be reiterated in a tidy little checklist in Appendix D, so relax and enjoy. Or turn directly to Appendix D and skip the rest of this chapter. Better yet, do both, minus the part about skipping the rest of this chapter.

Early abstinence for drug addicts and alcoholics is called *white-knuckling it*—gripping the arms of a chair to keep from using. Substance-dependent people know they won't progress in recovery if they don't keep addictive substances out of their bodies, because the introduction of the substance triggers craving. So, with a lot of help from peers who have attained sobriety, they white-knuckle it for the first few weeks or months by going to twelve-step meetings, hanging out with their sponsors, socializing with sober people rather than "using" friends, and avoiding toxic circumstances. What is the corollary for misery addicts? What does *using* look like for them?

Self put-downs

In the act of putting herself down or denigrating herself, the misery addict is using. Here's an example, when my younger son was six, my mother came to visit for a few weeks. One morning, she offered to fix breakfast. After mixing the pancake batter with my portable electric mixer, she ejected the beaters into the sink and, in so doing, dropped the whole mixer on the floor. An "el cheapo" gadget that probably had cost all of $4.98, it shattered completely! Mom murmured under her breath, "Grandma's always doing dumb things like that." My son asked me later, "Why does Grandma always put herself down?"

Fast-forward twenty-six years. I was visiting the same son—grown, married, and with a son of his own. While drying dishes one day, I dropped a saucer and broke it. "I'm always doing dumb stuff like that," I muttered. My son said, "Mom, you're putting yourself down exactly like Grandma used to." Talk about small events making big impressions!

Today, I consider self put-downs and retrospective faultfinding to be using. I abstain by consciously and deliberately refusing to shame, second-guess, or consign myself to purgatory when I make a mistake.

Another martyring behavior is being overly deferential. Full of self-doubt and insecurity, Naomi places herself in a one-down position in most social situations. One of the ways she goes about it is to be extremely apologetic. While she was in codependency treatment, her therapist put her on an apologizing blackout. One day she slipped into her "sorry" mode and was chided for it, whereupon she apologized for apologizing! Her apologetic attitude was self-deprecating. People close to her were annoyed by it. It's OK to take responsibility for our blunders, but we don't have to apologize for our very existence! Being overly apologetic can be a form of using.

Taking offense

This involves mind reading and assuming insults where they may or may not exist. Taking things people say or do personally without asking them for clarification before we jump to negative conclusions is using.

Vonda, a negaholic investment counselor with several months of sobriety from misery addiction, described an incident that indicated real growth: "In a departmental meeting yesterday, I made a lighthearted joke at my own expense. One of my colleagues picked up the punch line and took it a step further with an added hint of sarcasm. For a second, I felt as if I had been slapped in the face. Then I paused and made a conscious decision not to interpret his words or intentions negatively." Now that's abstinence!

Attention grabbing

The unfortunate thing about attention grabbing is that most misery addicts do it unconsciously. They don't realize they're whining and complaining, much less that they're doing it to garner attention. They're liable to be shocked and hurt if anyone mentions that they are oozing their neediness.

Attention seeking is difficult to confront, because the very attempt to make the martyr aware of what she is doing satisfies her need to be persecuted, which reinforces her negative attitude. Yech—just what we *don't* want to do. The person who really deserves sympathy is the therapist (in this case, me) who is struggling to teach the misery addict new behavior. Most efforts to point out attention-seeking behavior fall on deaf ears. They are, in fact, counterproductive. Pardon me while I indulge in a moment of self-pity. On second thought, I'll pass.

Gloom, doom, and despair

There are two activities that feed gloom and doom: worrying or "gerbiling" (going around and around in our heads trying to figure something out) and "awfulizing" (overgeneralizing, assuming the worst). The result? A totally infuriatingly hopeless and helpless attitude. Dr. Chérie Carter-Scott, international authority on overcoming negativity, labels people who do this as "help-rejecting complainers."[2] They lure caretakers into a trap by obsessing out loud about their problems and then rejecting or refusing to accept suggestions when they are offered.

Help-rejecting complainers deflect advice and argue with people who try to help them. The minute anyone offers a viable solution to their dilemma, they leap to the other side of the question and begin to debate them. Carmen is a classic example. Both her mother and grandmother rewarded her from her earliest years for being a problem child. Her never-ending difficulties provided Mom and Grandma with constant crises which they thrived on. Revolving around Carmen gave them a sense of meaning and purpose. Carmen's attention-seeking behavior worked so well for her that she continued being the official family problem child well into adulthood.

Help-rejecting complainers, according to Carter-Scott, learn early on that they will receive much more attention for getting hurt, being sick, not cleaning their plates, leaving their bedrooms messy, getting into trouble, telling lies, and being difficult rather than behaving well. With repeated imprinting, they internalize a motivational system whereby they receive attention for the negatives rather than the positives. Their addiction to negativity is based on the physiological, chemical rush they experience every time they engage in negative thoughts, words, or actions.[3]

Carmen got into one mess after another. She was always in trouble, always needing to be rescued. She collected caretakers—used them up, wore them out, and moved on to another. The harder her friends tried to help her, the more intractable her problems became. Every attempt to provide her with an answer to her current dilemma was skillfully rebutted. She played "Why don't you?— Yes, but . . ." constantly—and she always won. Here's how it sounded.

Carmen: "I'm so unhappy in my marriage. Maybe I should leave my husband."

Caretaker: "Maybe you should."

Carmen: "I really can't leave because I couldn't possibly support myself financially."

Caretaker: "Well, you could get a job."

Carmen: "There's no way I could get a job because I gave up my nursing career when I got married, and I don't have a current license."

Caretaker: "Maybe you could renew your license."

Carmen: "I could never meet the requirements because I haven't worked in ten years."

Caretaker: "Why don't you take a refresher course? I'm sure they're available."

Carmen: "I don't have the money to take a class."

Caretaker: "Maybe you could borrow it."

Carmen: "I could never qualify for a loan because I don't have a credit rating in my name only. The system conspires against women."

Caretaker: "I give up."

Obviously, because of the way her problematic behavior was reinforced in childhood, Carmen is not looking for answers. She just wants to be the center of attention. After the designated caretaker plays "Why don't you?— Yes, but . . ." with Carmen for a few minutes, all bets are off. The helper screams, "Wait a minute. Whose side are you on?"

Well-meaning friends and family are easily hooked into this kind of maddening game. To abstain from attention-seeking behavior, misery addicts need to ask for and accept input from others without debating them. Abstinence for martyr/caregivers is to abstain from rushing in and making suggestions unless asked and—even when asked—to detach themselves emotionally and let go of expectations as soon as the advice has been offered. Cut the strings immediately.

Self-sabotage

Isolation is a huge issue for misery addicts. They cannot ask for what they need when they are feeling hurt, lonely, or scared. In most cases, they don't even know what they want or need. Instead, they go off in a corner and try to wrestle their demons single-handedly.

The immature coping mechanisms they employ are many: self-harm, self-neglect, suicidal threats, smoking, drinking, drugging, and overeating, to name a few. Helen, an adult child of addiction and abuse, describes her experience in these words:

In the course of my childhood, I didn't have anyone to turn to for help when I felt bad. I stuffed my feelings deep inside, hoping they would vanish into the emptiness of my being, only to have them surface in self-harming behaviors (cutting myself or getting drunk).

As an adult, I'm still faced with the tendency to isolate myself. I avoid people who could give me love and support. I fight the idea of asking for help. I've built a wall separating my soul from the connections so desperately needed by all those who live. Isolation and depression nearly cost me my life. Instead of reaching out to others, I suffer alone and externalize my pain through self-harming behaviors. When I'm caught up in the blackness of isolation, I refuse to connect with others when I need them most. I refuse to get the light needed to find my way home.

Other self-sabotaging behaviors include failing to plan or prepare for specific events, failing to meet deadlines at work or school, refusing to attempt difficult challenges, deliberately breaking rules, or tempting fate. I know a young man who was sent back to prison after being released because he failed to report to his parole officer on schedule. When asked if he was aware of his appointments, he said Yes. I'd call that self-sabotage, wouldn't you?

Indecision: a decision to remain miserable

Another self-sabotaging behavior is sitting on the fence—remaining stuck in indecision or inaction for fear of making a mistake. T. Boone Pickens calls this the "ready, aim, aim, aim" syndrome. In reality, the discomfort of fence-sitting (picture a picket fence) is probably worse than the pain of making a mistake, but don't ask the misery addict to budge. It might require her to take action that would make her feel better, and we can't have that!

Indecisive misery addicts sell themselves short. They give up before they start. They allow their fear of failure to sabotage their success. Abstinence for such individuals is moving forward in the face of fear—faking it until they make it, if necessary. As Yogi Berra put it, "When you come to a fork in the road, take it."

Recovery is about change

Twenty-year-old Luke shared a major triumph with me recently: "My rageaholic father called last night and started dumping a load of shame on me. I deflected his abuse for the first time in my life. I didn't take it personally, even though he was attacking me unfairly. Instead of apologizing for something I wasn't guilty of, which is old behavior for me, I told him I had to go to class and hung up." Luke maintained strong internal boundaries. He didn't allow his father's raving to affect his self-esteem or change his mood.

If Luke *had* been distressed by his dad's verbal abuse, he could have used several recovery tactics or tools to keep from sinking into discouragement. He could have called his sponsor, shared what happened, and asked for support. He could have used positive affirmations to console the hurt little boy inside him who is still longing for Daddy's approval. Or he could have gone to a twelve-step meeting and received healthy fathering and brothering from the men in the group to compensate for what his father was incapable of giving him. He could also have generalized on the incident and asked the people at the meeting to discuss how they handle similar kinds of hurt and disappointment. Twelve-step groups provide nonjudgmental suggestions and support for these kinds of situations—no strings attached.

Putting the cork in the proverbial bottle

I'd like to recommend a few other forms of abstinence:

- Bypass the opportunity to complain whenever you can, and then celebrate your progress.
- Consciously choose a positive interpretation of a dubious situation instead of a negative one—give the other person the benefit of the doubt.
- Before jumping to conclusions, do a reality check with the individual involved. Let him speak for himself instead of buying into your own subjective interpretation.
- Refrain from overanalyzing people and circumstances.

When negaholics overanalyze anything, they invariably think themselves into perdition. Instead, let trustworthy people, such as your sponsor and recovering peers, think for you. Ask them to obsess on your behalf. You will be better served by seeking and accepting good orderly direction from objective sources outside your own brain and body than by wrestling with your demons alone.

Other abstinence measures include the following:

- Not feeling guilty for feeling good or for taking care of yourself
- Forgiving yourself *before* making a mistake—accepting your humanity
- Accepting the forgiveness of God and people when you err
- Refusing to beat yourself up when your performance isn't up to par
- Allowing yourself to relax and have fun
- Celebrating who you *are*—not what you do or how well you do it

Incidentally, I had to abstain from negativism in order to write this chapter because I had a martyr monkey sitting on my shoulder taunting me with thoughts such as, "people already know this stuff," "they're not interested," and "make sure you don't bore the readers." That is exactly what my father said when I entered my first writing contest at the age of sixteen. Old habits of thinking die hard, don't they?

Effective catharsis versus futile complaining

Martyrs need to know how to differentiate between effective catharsis, which is good, and futile complaining, which is "using." When I was in therapy, my counselor told me that every time a person shares a negative feeling, he cuts it in half, and every time he shares a positive feeling, he doubles it. Sharing our burdens reduces their weight. Celebrating our triumphs increases the joy.

That did not jibe with what I had been taught. In parochial school, I was told that *expression* deepens *impression*. I was informed that people shouldn't let their feelings govern them or get the best of them. So which is true? Should we share negative feelings or not?

Today, I believe that we are governed by *repressed* feelings—not by feelings that are expressed in healthy ways. Sharing a feeling with a safe person reduces its power to dominate our thinking and makes it less likely that we will behave irrationally. Here's an interesting example: Kim, a young teacher, was getting ready for school one day when she realized that she was fantasizing about grabbing the principal by his collar and punching him in the nose. She was angry at him for something that had happened the previous day, but her bizarre fantasy was disproportionate to the situation.

Instead of trying to analyze her attitude, Kim tried something her counselor had suggested—she stopped thinking about it and expressed the anger physically. Grabbing her son's Wiffle ball bat, she flailed on a pillow for about ten seconds, shouting, "I'm angry! I'm angry!" This discharged her emotional energy and freed her to be more objective.

Almost immediately, she realized that she wasn't angry at her *current* employer. She liked him and considered him a personal friend. She was angry at her former boss. The brief but dramatic outburst Kim permitted herself to have in private helped her detach herself from the irrational impulse to punch the principal in the nose. She recognized the real problem and gained the perspective she needed.

Recently, I was talking with a group of clients about cutting their negative feelings in half by sharing them with a safe person, when one of the clients—a brilliant law student—challenged me. The nerve of him! "I'm confused," he said. "You made the opposite point yesterday when you were lecturing about misery addiction. You said that negaholics should abstain from complaining. So what's the difference? How do we distinguish between sharing negative feelings to get relief and complaining to get attention?"

"Er, um, ah," said I. And I concluded my hemming and hawing with a resounding, "Duh. That's an excellent question. Let me think about it. I'll give you an answer tomorrow." Here's my reply: "Your misery addiction is flourishing when you would rather talk about a problem than solve it. Sharing negative emotions reduces their intensity, but that's only the beginning. We can't stop there. We have to move on to problem solving. As Edwin Lewis Cole puts it, 'You don't drown by falling in the water; you drown by staying there.' Any more questions?" I made this nifty little chart to compare effective sharing with futile complaining. I hope it helps to clarify the issue.

Effective Sharing

Definition: Owning your problem while seeking good, orderly direction from safe people.

Motive:
1. To get help, guidance, support
2. To detach yourself from irrational thinking
3. To move forward in your life

Behaviors:
1. Taking responsibility for self
2. Experiencing feelings while sharing them
3. Engaging in genuine catharsis—grieving, feeling *sorrow* for oneself
4. Asking directly for specific help
5. Freeing yourself from worry and woe

Outcomes:
1. Relief of stress
2. Energy to change
3. Serenity, peace of mind
4. A realistic action plan
5. Freedom from compulsion
6. Freedom to forgive
7. Renewed confidence in self and others

Futile Complaining

Definition: Handing your problem off to another person, expecting him or her to fix it.

Motive:
1. To get attention, affection, approval
2. To solicit sympathy
3. To massage the problem but still hang on to it

Behaviors:
1. Taking a passive stance (victim)
2. Feelings are absent or constricted, limited to helpless weeping or whining
3. Feeling sorry for oneself
4. Asking without asking (hinting)
5. Recycling misery, thus maintaining the "stash" of worry and woe for later use

Outcomes:
1. Temporary psychiatric high, followed by feeling worse instead of better
2. Addiction to misery is rewarded and reinforced
3. Nothing is solved or changed
4. Distrust of humankind is confirmed
5. Self-doubt is deepened

Sustainable change

Recovery is an inside job. It's not so much about changing outward behavior as it is about changing the deep-seated attitudes and beliefs that generate behavior. In Old Testament scripture, the prophet Jeremiah was pessimistic about the possibility of this kind of change. He asked rhetorically whether a person could change the color of his or her skin or whether a leopard could change its spots.[4]

Frequently, our attempts at self-improvement are superficial and unsuccessful, but that doesn't mean we should give up. I believe that all efforts at self-improvement are productive—even those that prove to be transitory and futile. Once we have exhausted our internal resources, we become willing to look for sources of strength and wisdom outside ourselves. Very few addicts are prepared to commit themselves to a rigorous program of character development until they are fully convinced that their own best efforts have failed and that no other option is available. Even our failed attempts to transform ourselves can be useful in that sense.

Alcoholics seem to have been among the first to recognize the futility of their own efforts and to seek more effective ways of solving seemingly insolvable problems. We turn now to these experts at failure to learn the humble lessons needed for sustainable recovery.

Hope for Today

The wise man said that there is wisdom in the counsel of numbers. This is the key to deep and lasting change—that, along with a remedial program of character development called the Twelve Steps. There's nothing new in these steps. They are a simple, strategic, sequential set of spiritual principles designed to help people discover the truth about who they are, what they do, and how they affect the people around them while—at the same time—learning from experience who God is, what God does, and how He affects human lives. In twelve-step fellowships, there is no dogma, and there are no requirements for membership, except a sincere desire to change and grow. That sounds like a very good place to start!

Self-Study

1. Do you know someone who uses complaining as a habitual conversation starter?
2. Have you ever lost the love and loyalty of a friend or family member because they got tired of listening to your problems?
3. When you realized that this person was becoming impatient with your complaining, did you try to be more upbeat? Did you succeed in changing your behavior?
4. Even if you failed, assure yourself that change is possible when you have the right tools.

---

1. Sexaholics Anonymous, *Sexaholics Anonymous* (n.p.: SA Literature, 1989), 4.

2. Chérie Carter-Scott, "Do You Live or Work With a Negaholic?" Negaholics.com, http://www.negaholics.com/live_with_a_negaholic.html.

3. Chérie Carter-Scott, *Negaholics* (New York: Fawcett-Columbine, 1996), 8.

4. See Jeremiah 13:23.

CHAPTER 11

Breaking the Cycle
of Worry and Woe

I believe in looking reality straight in the eye and denying it.

— Garrison Keillor

At this point, the prospect of trying to break the cycle of worry and woe may seem daunting. The good news is that, although recovery is not easy, it's simple. The remedial program of identity, personality, and character development that works for alcoholics works for misery addicts too. For most die-hard misery addicts, the hardest part to accept is the fact that it's such a simple program. Victims and martyrs have a difficult time getting excited about anything that doesn't promise to be agonizingly difficult! "Please, no . . . I can handle only *impossible* tasks!"

Before we delve into the process of how to make deep, lasting change, let's look at a few cognitive and behavioral techniques that are worth trying. They fall into the "just do it" category.

Addiction specialists discovered long ago that the just-do-it plan works better for people who aren't fully addicted than it does for full-blown, late-stage addicts. The success rate for applying sheer willpower to drinking problems, for example, is higher for social drinkers than it is for gutter drunks.

If you try to apply the techniques I'm about to suggest, the worst thing that could happen is that you won't succeed. For example, if you try to stop thinking negatively, you may find yourself doing it even more. If you try to stop assuming that everyone is against you, you won't be able to convince yourself that this is true. If you resolve to quit complaining, you'll catch yourself complaining in spite of your best intentions. But this, in itself, will add to your diagnostic data, motivate you to try something different, and increase your readiness for the simple program called the Twelve Steps, which has an excellent track record. More on that subject later.

What we're facing

Misery addicts are dealing with long-standing, deep-seated habits of thinking, believing, and behaving. Any decent negaholic can amass a pile of worries, stir them around in her head until they congeal into a gelatinous mass, dump the whole mess into the black hole of despair, and jump in after it in fifteen seconds or less.

If you happen to be in the geographical area while a misery addict is obsessing, beware. There's a magnetic field around him or her that draws onlookers into the black hole. Healthy people run the other direction as soon as they feel the magnetic pull. About the eighteenth time the misery addict sees a friend's backside disappear around the corner, she begins to realize that her behavior is driving people out of her life.

So just do it—if you can

From colleagues, clients, and personal experience, I've gathered the following suggestions for behavioral change. If you can put them into practice, great; if not, it's OK. There is a backup plan.

Demolish your worries

Here are some tools for dismantling your worries. First, take a lesson from Scarlett O'Hara: wait to worry. History would suggest that most worrying is futile anyway, so why not just postpone it? Make an appointment to obsess about your problems after you get off work today. Meanwhile, table them. Or write them on slips of paper and put them in a "God box." Nine chances out of ten, your problems will solve themselves before the day is over.

If the worrisome thoughts keep returning, distract yourself. Sing. Pray. Take a short walk. Do jumping jacks. Lift weights. Laugh. Repeat affirmations. Memorize a poem or a Bible verse. Plan a treat for yourself or someone you love.

Suggestion two: let someone else worry on your behalf. I'm serious. Ask three to five of your peers for good, orderly direction, and then go with the majority. Other people are more objective about your issues than you are, and their brains will probably work better and faster than yours. They will come up with more useful suggestions in three minutes than you could conjure up in three hours of obsessing.

Asking a jury of your peers to help you solve a problem is much more efficient than trying to do it alone. Be sure that the jury is made up of people who don't have an agenda for you—a selfish interest in the outcome.

There's a saying in recovery circles that every time an addict goes into his own mind, he's behind enemy lines. In other words, your mind is programmed for self-destruction. So don't go there! If you want to avoid getting mugged, stay out of dangerous neighborhoods! Instead of obsessing about your problems, ask for guidance from a few healthy friends.

Here's another suggestion: focus on what's going on in your heart instead of your head. One of the best ways to stop ruminating is to face the very thing you've been avoiding—your feelings. Feelings, the little "brain" in your stomach, can be very informative.

When you're in a spin cycle of self-analysis, you're going nowhere. I call this *obsessive overanalyzing.* It's impossible to think your way out of your feelings. It's far more effective to embrace them—face the pain, shame, fear, or anger you've been trying not to acknowledge. Express them in written form: a letter to God as you understand God, a letter (that you won't send) to the person(s) you're afraid of or angry at, a letter of empathy to yourself. This may help you grieve. Showing compassion for yourself, expressing sympathy to the childlike part of yourself that feels scared and alone, is not the same as self-pity. It is legitimate grief.

Feelings have been described as "energy in motion." You can move your feelings up and out by verbalizing them, but be careful to express *feelings*—not *opinions*. There is a difference. Expressing thoughts can contribute to further rumination and confusion. Expressing feelings is cleansing.

The best catharsis results from allowing yourself to experience and express the pain, fear, or anger by screaming, crying, or pounding your fists on a pillow in a safe setting. Before you dismiss this as the silliest idea you've ever heard, try it! You'll get better results from an expressive exercise of this kind than you will from overthinking the situation.

Simply pause long enough to consult yourself and find out what you're feeling hurt, scared, sad, or angry about. Then find a private place where you can unload your emotional baggage. (The ideal environment for this kind of cathartic work is in a therapy group with an experienced facilitator. Such experiential groups can be found through counseling agencies and treatment centers. Many individual therapists conduct them.)

Once you have released your anger energy, breathe deeply and wait for the insight to come. This may surprise you, but you will "see" your illogic more quickly and more clearly if you embrace the feelings involved than if you obsess strenuously for the same amount of time. Somehow, clearing the negative energy out of yourself makes room for positive thoughts and feelings to flow in.

For those who are already in a twelve-step program, this is a good time to do a mini-fourth step on the issue you're struggling with and share it with your sponsor. Step Four will be discussed further in chapter 13.

Set boundaries

Sooner or later, martyrs have to stop accepting the unacceptable. If they don't, they will continue to be victimized. When you empower yourself to act in your own best interests, you step out of the victim role. Therapy groups and individual counselors can help you develop the skill and ability to establish and maintain healthy boundaries—to stand up and speak up on your own behalf. A leading expert on stress reduction says that underassertiveness is a frequent cause of stress, anxiety, and a sense of helplessness.[1] Hear! Hear!

The magic word here is *empowerment*. Abusers don't stop abusing victims just because the victim cries, begs, or pleads for mercy. Abusers don't stop abusing victims when the victims become compliant and try to satisfy their demands. They don't stop when victims reason with them or prove from the Bible that they shouldn't be hurting them. Abusers don't stop when victims utter empty threats and ultimatums. They don't stop abusing until victims refuse to accept abuse.

A recovering alcoholic with a long history of battering women told his pastor that he had beaten his first two wives but not his third. When the pastor asked him why he didn't abuse her, he replied, "Because I knew she wouldn't put up with it."

Now, given the fact that accepting the unacceptable is a symptom of misery addiction, we must take responsibility for change by learning how to establish and maintain boundaries. Gaining the boundary-setting skills necessary to step out of the victim role is a big job. It will require a serious commitment to therapy and appropriate support groups. It may also require knowing when, where, and how fast to run.

Trying to hold your ground and protect your rights (as in "I'm not going to let him drive *me* out of town") is an insane kind of martyring if you are dealing with someone who is out of control and/or mentally ill. I could tell story after story about people who were determined to protect their property or their investments, women who stood their ground and refused to abandon their homes or jobs when they were being threatened. They ended up sacrificing their lives or the life of a son or daughter because of their stubbornness—or their addiction to misery.

Practice healthy self-care

In terms of the physiological aspects of overcoming chronic negativity, misery addicts need to look at lifestyle habits such as diet, exercise, sleep, etc. By all means, take note of diet-induced mood swings and make necessary adjustments. Too much caffeine, as little as one and a half to three cups of coffee a day, increases anxiety and stress significantly. Nicotine stimulates the anxiety cycle. Too much sugar can contribute to depression, as can certain food additives.

Extreme dieting or anorexic behavior depletes serotonin, one of the brain's feel-good chemicals. Lack of adequate vitamins and minerals can affect the nervous system negatively. Misery addicts must take care of themselves physically. This means—at the very least—taking a good multivitamin and getting plenty of B vitamins and omega-3s in your diet.

Exercise is another important issue. It releases endorphins that enhance a person's sense of well-being. Your moods will improve drastically if you fit thirty to sixty minutes of aerobic exercise into your routine at least every other day. Some psychiatrists say that exercise is as potent an antidepressant as antidepressant medication.

Don't misunderstand me. If you are on medication, I'm not suggesting that you replace your prescriptions with exercise. Do both! Speaking of which, I encourage you to consult a reputable psychiatrist to see if anxiolytic or antidepressant medication might be indicated in your case. Remember Daniel Goleman's statement: "When one's emotions are of great intensity and linger past an appropriate point, they shade over into their distressing extremes—chronic anxiety, uncontrollable rage, depression. And, at their most severe and intractable, medication, psychotherapy, or both may be needed to lift them."[2]

I encourage all misery addicts to access nutritional guidance, medical support, and inpatient treatment or psychological counseling. Don't make recovery harder than it needs to be. Trying to do it on your own is difficult, plus it's a symptom of martyring. Bear in mind that even though medical support is vital, pills are not the total answer. Developing mature coping skills is just as important. It's OK to start by working on skill development, but remember that both pills *and* skills are often needed.

Other basics

In their book, *Overcoming Anxiety, Panic, and Depression,* James Gardiner, MD, and Allen H. Bell, PhD, suggest gardening, communing with nature, playing with a pet, enjoying art and music, meditating and prayer, talking to a trusted person, getting a massage, and employing relaxation and biofeedback strategies as ways to overcome negativity.[3] Along with these simple strategies, they also suggest living in the present, simplifying your schedule, making fewer demands on yourself, focusing on the things that matter most, and slowing down. No more rushing around.[4] Don't even rush past this paragraph. Pause and consider how you could implement these suggestions. Make a plan and commit to it.

One of the first things I had to do to put these ideas into practice was to abstain from multitasking! Whenever I try to do several things at once, my adrenaline goes sky high and so does my blood pressure. Now I walk around every day, muttering, "One thing at a time, Carol. One thing at a time."

Banishing unhealthy shame and neurotic guilt

Few spiritual burdens are greater than that of unhealthy shame. What's the difference between healthy shame and unhealthy shame? Healthy shame shows us that we're human and therefore imperfect. It makes us aware of what is socially appropriate and what isn't. It helps keep our behavior within reasonable boundaries. One expert says that people need just enough shame to keep them from running through the supermarket naked!

John Bradshaw defines healthy shame as an awareness of one's human condition—a recognition of one's limitations. Everyone needs a certain amount of this kind of shame. By contrast, unhealthy shame is a brooding state of being that refuses to be relieved. It is not about how we *feel,* but about who we think we *are* (as in "the scum of the earth"). Shame-based people feel flawed, defective, worthless, and stupid.

Healthy *guilt* is a different matter. We feel guilty when we violate our own ethical code or what we understand God's moral code to be. Bear in mind that God's rules can be easily confused with Dad's rules and the mandates of other authority figures. Learning to distinguish between God's requirements and man-made rules will take time. The confusion will sort itself out with time and plenty of good, orderly direction from healthy mentors. In any case, when we err, our guilt leads us to regret our behavior while still respecting ourselves. When we admit our mistake and make amends, the guilt has served its purpose, and it goes away. It doesn't linger.

Unhealthy shame and guilt are the products of a conscience that has been programmed to a high degree of perfectionism. No amount of amends making will relieve people of unhealthy guilt or shame, because they are convinced that they can never be good enough. People with unhealthy shame suffer under the lash of constant self-criticism, which can lead to self-defeating or self-destructive behaviors, such as martyring.

Guilt is not meant to be an instrument of self-torture, and shame is not meant to immobilize us. Healthy shame provides us with humility and restraint, and guilt motivates us to correct our mistakes and refrain from repeating them. A healthy measure of guilt and shame can be helpful, but an undue burden of either is deadly.

If you're a misery addict, your burden of unhealthy shame and guilt must be removed through amends making. This is a delicate matter and must be approached carefully with the guidance of sponsors who have walked the path ahead of you. Otherwise, you will do more harm than good when you try to make amends. The best path, in my opinion, is the Twelve Steps, which provides a sequential way of dealing with your past mistakes. Without a program of this kind, you will be at risk for riding the pendulum back and forth from one extreme to the other. As they say, 180 degrees from sick is still sick.

Take aggressive action

Another abstinence measure is to run from the valley of indecision and inaction. With the help of viable sources of wisdom and strength, tease out a single issue from the obsessive mass rolling around in your head, make a list of options, consult objective sources of wisdom, turn the problem over to your Higher Power, and pray for a knowledge of God's will and the power to carry it out. Then create an action plan, surrender the outcome to God, and implement your plan immediately, leaving the results to your Higher Power. Don't procrastinate. Procrastination is the highest form of self-sabotage.

Having surrendered the situation to the God of your understanding, you may be tempted to meddle or try to force the outcome. Don't. The results are out of your hands. The outcome is none of your business. If you find that the decision you made was less than perfect, you can make midstream corrections or you can simply learn from your mistakes. Mistakes are not sins punishable by death. They are simply learning opportunities.

Find a spiritual home

For many recovering people, the first spiritual home they find is a twelve-step group. They feel comfortable there because they sense that the atmosphere is nonjudgmental, noncritical, and noncontrolling. Some would call this a fellowship of common suffering.

According to James Nelson, retired professor of Christian ethics and a recovering alcoholic, recovering people have diverse religious and non-religious backgrounds, and some of them carry lasting religious damage. For this reason, he says they may need to begin their spiritual journey in a neutral place. "A more generalized 'spiritual' approach is utterly appropriate," he adds.[5] Amen.

In his book, *Thirst: God and the Alcoholic Experience,* Nelson suggests that because many alcoholics and addicts carry a heavy load of guilt and shame, they instinctively shy away from anyone who would add more to that burden. "Few alcoholics are able to experience divine grace directly," he says. "Shame-based people need something en-fleshed, concrete. Many find a crucial incarnation of grace in recovery groups."[6] The blessings of church fellowship cannot replace or fully replicate this, and that's OK.

It's important for recovering addicts who have been spiritually abused to take adequate time determining if and when they feel safe enough to venture beyond the twelve-step group. Before they are ready to return to the church of their choice, they need to be mature and secure enough not to slip into obsessive religiosity as a substitute for their original addiction. We call this "switching addictions."

Using obsessive religious practices or disciplines to avoid the grinding responsibility of growing up and getting healthy is very tempting. People with addictive personalities are capable of turning almost anything into an addiction—even good things such as religion, health, relationships, hobbies, and exercise.

Once misery addicts have (a) addressed their issues of immaturity through therapy, (b) grown themselves up by using the process of identity, personality, and character development that we will discuss in chapter 13, and (c) established strong internal boundaries—the ability to maintain their sense of value regardless of how others treat them—they may wish to reestablish contact with organized religion and find a church home that will help them maintain their spiritual growth. I highly recommend exploring spiritual or religious belief systems and finding safe places to worship when the time is right.

What is a "safe church"? Safe churches provide a nurturing, nonjudgmental, noncontrolling environment. They support experimentation, exploration, and personal choice. The leaders and members are secure enough to accept people who are in their spiritual "adolescence" and allow them to grow one day at a time without shaming them unduly or exhorting them constantly. They don't try to rush them. Ideally, they also have an understanding of addiction and codependence and sincere faith in twelve-step programs.

And if you can't...

If you can't follow these suggestions for behavioral change consistently, you are at Step One, which is not a bad place to be, "We admitted we were powerless over our addiction to misery [negative thinking, complaining, worrying, etc.], that our lives had become unmanageable."

The very idea that one must surrender to win—admit complete defeat in order to gain enduring strength—is a paradox. Many people find the notion of powerlessness incomprehensible if not downright offensive. They view it as a kind of defeatism or blind resignation. But it is neither. There is a vast difference between succumbing to one's weakness and surrendering to one's need of help—a worthy subject for further examination.

Summary

I'm going to summarize the major points in this chapter so they don't fall through the cracks. I have suggested two approaches to recovery from misery addiction. One is behavioral, and the other is spiritual. Both approaches are legitimate, and each can be effective to a greater or lesser extent.

The cognitive or behavioral approach includes such things as abstinence from complaining, refusing to whine, waiting to worry, asking safe people for objective input, eating a healthful diet, getting abundant exercise, practicing relaxation techniques, journaling, having a psychiatric evaluation, taking medication if indicated, setting healthy boundaries, refusing to be victimized, staying out of the valley of indecision, engaging in prayer and meditation, and networking for nurturance and support via church and twelve-step groups. Nothing new or unusual here.

For certain negaholics, some of these tasks may be hard to achieve. For others, not so much. Many recovery-seekers have trouble making changes. There may be a number of reasons for this. Perhaps there are underlying issues that have yet to be addressed. Therapy may be needed.

Twelve-step groups are an excellent adjunct to therapy. They provide the nurturing and guidance addicts need in order to grow up and become responsible adults. They offer a safe, confidential place where recovering people can discover a process, a set of principles, and a Higher Power that will do for them what they cannot do for themselves. How to access and benefit from these God-given resources will be the subject of the next two chapters.

Hope for Today

Addicts and codependents, who face challenges bigger than themselves and try desperately to "gain the victory," are amazed to discover that admitting failure is a relief. Misery addicts have to recognize and accept the impossibility of their situation before they will ask for help. As long as they persist in battering themselves against the proverbial brick wall, trying to break through, they are not only destined to fail, but they are also doing unnecessary harm to themselves—bludgeoning their bodies and souls—and thus weakening an already compromised condition. There is a better alternative.

Self-Study

1. Do a simple experiment: try brushing your teeth three times a day for two days with the opposite hand from the one you usually use.
2. The next time you catch yourself habitually worrying or obsessing, formulate your concern into a simple problem statement and ask a friend to help you solve it. Notice how much more efficient this approach is.
3. Write four affirmations based on the material you read in this

chapter, such as "Today, I will wait to worry"; "I can ask directly for what I need"; and "I am a courageous person."

---

1. Archibald Hart, *The Hidden Link Between Adrenaline and Stress* (Dallas: Word Publishing, 1995), 106.

2. Daniel Goleman, *Emotional Intelligence,* 57, 58.

3. James Gardiner and Arthur H. Bell, *Overcoming Anxiety, Panic, and Depression* (Franklin Lakes, N.J.: Career Press, 2000), 182.

4. Ibid., 185.

5. James B. Nelson, *Thirst: God and the Alcoholic Experience* (Louisville: Westminster John Knox Press, 2004), 6.

6. Ibid., 22.

CHAPTER 12

The Twelve Steps Aren't for People Who Don't Need Them

Man blames fate for other accidents but feels
personally responsible for a hole-in-one.

— Martha Beckman

We all have idiosyncrasies that frustrate us and irritate our significant others. Have you ever tried to change one of those annoying little habits and failed? Maybe you promised yourself you would stop interrupting people, snapping your gum, biting your nails, or talking too loud, because you knew how much it bugged people. You really tried to stop. When that didn't work, you *really* tried. And, when that didn't work, you *really, really* tried.

Even if your negativity doesn't seem to bother anyone else, you know it's hurting you, so you've made many sincere attempts to stop complaining, seeking attention, or expecting people to fix you. But, in spite of your best intentions, you still catch yourself doing the very things you don't want to do. You're in good company. The apostle Paul had the same problem.[1]

Most people resolve at least once a year to make major or minor changes in their lives, only to discover that *deciding* to behave differently does not always produce the desired results. No matter how hard they try or cry or beg or plead or pray, they remain stuck in old habit patterns.

The good news is that there is another way to change long-standing, deep-seated habits—a set of simple, practical, spiritual principles that can be applied to any number of unhealthy behaviors. The principles evolved from a chance conversation between two falling-down drunks, who had failed repeatedly in their efforts to abstain from drinking and had nearly given up. These two men with feet of clay didn't know that the lives of millions of people would be changed by the solution they stumbled upon.

The model for change they discovered is not superficial. It isn't magic, and it can't be accomplished overnight. It is a gradual, gentle approach to growth and healing that brings out the best in people—helps them become all that they were meant to be. This program, known as the Twelve Steps, is a strategic, sequential set of spiritual principles that help people live peaceful, serene, successful lives, whether or not they have ever had a problem with alcohol. Is it appropriate for everyone? No. The Twelve Steps are only for people who need them.

Legitimate concerns

Many individuals have reservations about twelve-step groups. Some think it's not OK to go for help to sources outside their home, family, or church. Sometimes these convictions are firmly rooted in the biases of previous generations. "Mom and Dad solved their problems without going to counselors or support groups, and I can too" is their logic. That's a perfectly acceptable approach to life. There's no need to change if it's working.

Some ultraconservative religious people suspect that twelve-step programs are a dangerous new gospel that conflicts with or is in competition with their deeply held religious beliefs. They're afraid that their beliefs will be compromised if they attend twelve-step groups. (They don't stop to think that their value system—and possibly their Christian witness as well—is *already* being compromised by the addictive and/or compulsive behavior they are engaging in.)

Have you heard the saying that people are down on what they aren't up on? Condemnation prior to investigation is an age-old problem. Most of us have trouble living up to our democratic ideal—innocent until proven guilty—in this regard.

Some religiously oriented folks object to the fact that twelve-step groups are not specific enough in defining God. They're uncomfortable with terms such as "Higher Power" and "God of our understanding." They don't realize that twelve-step groups deliberately use such terminology in order to open the door of welcome wide enough so that anyone who has a desire to abstain from addictive behavior can find the help and hope they need.

The irony of this is that some *alcoholics* avoid AA because they consider it too religious, and other alcoholics avoid it because they think it's not religious enough! There may be deeper reasons for their reluctance, but every individual has to work through his own personal reservations in his own time. Wisdom and insight can't be hurried. I usually suggest that newcomers to twelve-step groups who still have reservations about their legitimacy attend six to twelve meetings, listening skeptically but with an open mind, before they make a decision.

Remember, twelve-step principles are not for people who don't need them. They're not for generic sinners who don't know what's wrong with them. They are for people who have been brought low by a sin, a substance, or a situation over which they have lost control. *They are for people who know that they are wretched, poor, blind, naked, and in need of help!*

One pilgrim's perspective

To anyone who is willing to examine the issues further before making a final judgment about twelve-step programs, I offer the following perspectives. In so doing, I am not speaking on behalf of any twelve-step organization, of which there are many. Nor am I claiming affiliation with any twelve-step group, although I have attended most of them. I am an ordinary person from a conservative religious background who has gone to twelve-step meetings for twenty-five years but who was *very* skeptical about them at first. I was one of the doubters.

The first thing I noticed when I began attending twelve-step meetings was that they leave the task of defining God to the individual. They do not preempt the place of church and religion in a person's life. While churches teach people what they consider to be the truth about God and how God affects their lives, twelve-step programs help people discover the truth about *themselves* and how they affect others. And they accomplish this in a manner that is respectful of the individual's existing religious beliefs.

Lloyd, a closet sex addict, hesitated to go to twelve-step meetings because his brother told him that he would just be trading one addiction for another. But when his addiction left him no choice but to seek help, he went to Sexaholics Anonymous. He sensed immediately that there was more to the Twelve Steps than meets the eye. While the meetings themselves provided him with strength and insight, it was the spiritual principles he learned there that made the difference.

It wasn't a matter of lamely depending on other people. The principles of the program helped Lloyd grow and mature as a person. He found a Higher Power with whom he could do business. He learned to relate to God and others in a more realistic, balanced way. He got honest with himself, made himself accountable for his behavior, and developed a closer connection to his wife and children. The changes in his life went far beyond mere abstinence from sexual acting out.

People who are struggling with a problem bigger than themselves and greater than all the resources they can muster from within themselves have an uncommon understanding of other people struggling with similar problems. They have a unique ability to guide and nurture them in the process of change. And they're able to do it in a nonjudgmental, nonthreatening way.

Have you ever thought about the fact that Jesus took a support group with Him wherever He went? Believers who are suffering from addictive disorders can safely follow His example. Before they can find relief from their addictions, however, some have to overcome their reluctance to reach out for help from people they consider different from themselves.

The fellowship of common suffering

The Twelve Steps were conceived in the 1930s by a group of down-and-out alcoholics who discovered that they could accomplish together what they could not achieve single-handedly. They learned that there was wisdom and strength in the counsel of numbers. The principles of the program grew out of a religious movement of the day—the Oxford Group. The original hundred or so alcoholics acknowledged with gratitude the fact that the spiritual keys by which they were liberated were given to them by men and women of faith. Today there are over one hundred thousand Alcoholics Anonymous groups in 150 countries with more than two million members.

Alcoholics Anonymous (AA) is designed for people who have a desire to stop drinking. Shortly after AA was founded, the friends and relatives of alcoholics began to meet together in an effort to deal with the frustrations of living with an alcoholic. They eventually formed Al-Anon Family Groups.[2] Like AA, Al-Anon is a worldwide fellowship today.

Narcotics Anonymous began in 1953. With AA's permission and blessing, NA based its program on AA's Twelve Steps with one simple modification: the word *alcohol* was changed to *addiction.* Narcotics Anonymous and its companion group, Nar-Anon, have flourished as much as have AA and Al-Anon.

Gamblers Anonymous was an outgrowth of a chance meeting between two men with a baffling history of trouble and misery due to an obsession with gambling. Founded in 1957, Gamblers Anonymous meetings are now available in many countries, as are corollary groups called Gam-Anon—for people affected by a loved one's gambling problem.

Overeaters Anonymous was formed in 1960 to support people dealing with the physical and emotional symptoms of compulsive eating. Another group for people suffering from eating disorders—Eating Disorders Anonymous—has evolved more recently.

The list of twelve-step groups goes on: in 1966, convinced that the Twelve Steps could be used as a tool for recovery from emotional illness, the first Emotions Anonymous group came into being. Other groups that followed suit include Sexaholics Anonymous and S-Anon, Co-Dependents Anonymous, Incest Survivors Anonymous, Debtors Anonymous, Workaholics Anonymous, and yes, even Misery Addicts Anonymous. I believe that the proliferation of twelve-step programs is a testimony to their effectiveness and a mark of God's blessing. Information on most of these organizations is provided in Appendix G.

Why are they necessary?

Through no fault of their own, people reared in painful, traumatized, dysfunctional, or addictive environments have had limited opportunities to develop character early in life. To the extent that they were deprived of adequate guidance and nurturing, they have been unable to complete their childhood developmental tasks.[3] They failed to mature and achieve a sense of identity and value. The growth and development of their personality was warped or twisted by the addiction and abuse in their lives.

Socially and emotionally challenged, such individuals need a remedial program of character, identity, and personality development. That's where twelve-step programs fit in. Twelve-step programs provide a simple, strategic, sequential set of principles—a practical model for addressing character defects and developmental deficits that is very respectful. "Working a program" means putting these principles into practice in daily life.

Comparable programs

In the educational setting, remedial classes are designed to help pupils with academic problems catch up to grade level. Whatever the subject, they provide a course of study intended to improve the student's skills, add to his knowledge, refresh his memory, and/or compensate for specific weaknesses or deficits. Ultimately, remedial programs are meant to prepare the student to advance to the next level of learning.

In medical terms, twelve-step programs can be compared to a "natural remedy." A natural remedy is noninvasive, nontoxic, readily available, relatively inexpensive, easily administered, gentle, and gradual. This could be said for twelve-step programs. In addition, personal trainers are part of the package—offered at no additional cost. Twelve-step groups provide sponsors to help new members understand and employ the principles of the program.

While the tools of the program (meetings, steps, sponsors, and service work) gradually relieve the compulsion to behave self-destructively, they also help people discover who they are, what they do, and why they do it. Participants become more aware of their own behavior, more cognizant of their motives. They take responsibility for themselves and their actions. The openness and honesty engendered breaks down barriers and creates genuine intimacy. The atmosphere is one of healthy interdependence.

Real people—real results

Juanita, a fifty-something professional woman who has been involved in Al-Anon for several years, says, "The Twelve Steps have become an integral part of my thinking. When I find myself struggling with insurmountable problems, I turn to the first three steps [I can't, God can, I think I'll let Him] for relief from worry. As soon as I surrender the problem, my stress levels drop. When my feelings are hurt, I no longer brood. Instead, I do a moral inventory [Step Four] to discover where *I* am at fault. When I look at situations through my twelve-step glasses, I gain a new perspective."

Daphne, a longtime member of Overeaters Anonymous, describes her personal experience: "I found in the Twelve Steps a practical way of applying the Christian principles I have always believed in. In the steps, surrender, faith, soul-searching, confession, transformation of character, accountability, prayer, meditation, and witnessing are placed in their proper order. As a result of practicing the steps on a daily basis, my relationships with self, God, and others have improved 100 percent."

Kevin, a recovering drug addict and father of two teenagers, states, "I was introduced to the Twelve Steps in 1997. Finding myself spiritually, physically, and emotionally bankrupt and nearing death, I began my spiritual journey. By working the steps, I have gained a relationship with God, serenity, self-acceptance, and an ability to love unconditionally."

Pete, a deeply depressed ACoA (adult child of alcoholism), says simply, "The Twelve Steps have given me a desire to live and not die. Thanks to the changes they have made in me, I now look forward to waking up every day."

Nancy, a recovering misery addict, describes how she benefited from working the steps: "I've learned that it's not the big problems in life that cause me to act out self-destructively. It's the little things. When I was actively drinking, I repeatedly let minor irritations drive me to the bottle. Now, if I am troubled about something, the Twelve Steps give me tools to pinpoint the problem and find a solution."

Finally, a pastor who grew up in an abusive workaholic and perfectionistic family system reports that his twelve-step program has taken him to a new level of spirituality: "Through working the steps, I have found a measure of self-understanding that allows me to relate to God and people in healthier ways. I have greater empathy for people who are struggling to survive. I am able to live a more balanced life and to share genuine experience, strength, and hope with others instead of empty, idealistic preachments."

For more than seventy years, Alcoholics Anonymous and other twelve-step fellowships have been a vehicle for bringing millions of suffering people out of death into life. Those who walk the twelve-step pathway do not limit their aspirations to mere abstinence. Many have found in these steps not only a daily reprieve from their addictions and compulsions but also a means to happy and effective living.

The next chapter will contain a practical description of the steps and how to do them. This is the starting point. Don't falter now. You're about to discover a tested and tried method for change—one that is almost too good to be true. Often when salesmen make this kind of pitch, they add a money-back guarantee. Here it is: twelve-step programs don't cost a penny, but your *misery* will be fully refunded if they don't work for you!

Hope for Today

The remedial program of character development portrayed in this chapter works for anyone who is struggling with an ill-gotten habit of thinking, believing, or behaving. If you have tried for an interminable period of time to change and found yourself unable to do so, you're in good company. The program, the principles, the people, and the process described above are very effective. The time and effort required for you to go to a twelve-step meeting will not be as great as the amount of time and effort you spend every day practicing self-defeating habits and then cleaning up the mess. Change is possible through the proven method of the Twelve Steps.

Self-Study

1. Is there a person or situation in your life that seems unmanageable? Have you made attempts to control the situation or the

way you react to it? How much is the problem upsetting you today?

2. Have you asked God to resolve or remove it? Has it magically disappeared?

3. Write a description of your current dilemma in no more than three sentences. Call a trusted friend and ask what he or she would do if he or she were in your shoes.

4. Now celebrate the fact that you just practiced the first three steps without knowing it. To learn more about these twelve steps, go to chapter 13.

---

1. See Romans 7:23.

2. The founding "mother" of Al-Anon was Lois W., wife of the founder of AA. Lois's grandparents were conservative Christians. One set of grandparents was Sabbath keepers, and the other set kept Sunday. In my opinion, some of the concepts of AA literature, especially those dealing with the will, reflect popular religious literature of the time. Note this familiar-sounding line from *The Twelve Steps and Twelve Traditions:* "It is when we try to make our will conform with God's that we begin to use it rightly. . . . *Our whole trouble has been the misuse of willpower. We had tried to bombard our problems with it instead of attempting to bring it into agreement with God's intention for us.* To make this increasingly possible is the purpose of AA's Twelve Steps." Alcoholics Anonymous, *The Twelve Steps and Twelve Traditions,* 40.

3. The basic developmental tasks are delineated in Appendix E, "The Eight Stages of Human Development."

CHAPTER 13

We *Do* Recover!

Sometimes I lie awake at night and ask, "Why me?" Then a voice
answers, "Nothing personal, your name just happened to come up."
— Charlie Brown

After I went through inpatient treatment for workaholism, one of the many gifts God gave me was the best sponsor east of the Mississippi. A long-standing tradition in twelve-step programs, sponsorship is designed to help the newcomer define and practice abstinence and guide him or her in the proper use of the tools of the program, in much the same way that a personal trainer would instruct a gym member in the proper use of the gym's equipment.

Active in several twelve-step groups, my sponsor had built a firm foundation for her own recovery in the literature of Alcoholics Anonymous, under the tutelage of an excellent sponsor. People who have themselves been well-sponsored make excellent sponsors of others.

I'd like to invite you to the first meeting I had with Tina two days after I got home from treatment. She greeted me kindly and handed me a little book, the *Twelve Steps and Twelve Traditions* (of Alcoholics Anonymous). Then she invited me to read aloud from the foreword. These were the words I read, "AA is a worldwide fellowship of . . . alcoholic men and women who are banded together to solve their common problems and to help fellow sufferers in recovery from that age-old, baffling malady, alco-holism."[1]

At that point, Tina asked me to pause, but she said nothing. The message sunk in. My workaholism, perfectionism, compulsive caregiv-ing, and control issues were maladies every bit as cunning, baffling, and powerful as alcoholism. "Keep reading," she said after a time of silence.

"This book deals with the 'Twelve Steps' and the 'Twelve Tradi-tions' of Alcoholics Anonymous. It presents an explicit view of the principles by which AA members recover. . . . AA's twelve steps are a group of principles, spiritual in their nature, which, if practiced as a way of life, can expel the obsession to drink and enable the sufferer to become happily and usefully whole."[2] In my own mind, I translated the word *drink* to "overdo anything." I had been overdoing many things—working, worrying, caregiving, controlling, managing, manipulating, etc.

"What do you need to do to recover?" Tina queried.

"Learn to practice these principles as a way of life," I replied. And we both paused to reflect deeply. I remain eternally grateful for that mo-ment. I knew I was home. I was standing on the front porch of a warm, welcoming place, and Tina had just handed me the key.

The empowering grace of powerlessness
Step One

The journey to wholeness begins with recognizing our need: "We ad-mitted we were powerless over misery addiction, that our lives had be-come unmanageable." Before we can abstain from complaining and de-tach ourselves from our worries and woes, we negaholics must realize that we are powerless in the face of our addictive beliefs and behaviors. We have to end our futile efforts to achieve the impossible and acknowl-edge our need of help.

Where the compulsion to self-sabotage is concerned, we win the war when we admit that we have lost the battle. As mentioned earlier, as long as we persist in battering ourselves against a brick wall, trying to break through, we are not only destined to fail, but we are doing undue harm to ourselves and weakening an already-compromised condition. By contrast, when we acknowledge that our problems are bigger than we are and greater than all the resources we can muster from within ourselves, we are in a position to get the help we need.

We'll never call for help and experience the desired break through if we think we have to do it on our own. When we take Step One, we're demonstrating the kind of honesty, open-mindedness, and willingness that makes us teachable. Although this is a humbling experience, it is also huge relief. Humility is the key.

While struggling to accept Step One, I went through the classic stages of grief—denial, anger, bargaining, depression, and acceptance. Addicted to caretaking, control, perfectionism, overworking, and misery, I was letting go of all the things that had made me the person I thought I was supposed to be. Saying, "I can't do this anymore" was extremely painful. Admitting that my best efforts had failed was agonizing. I felt as if I were dying.

Step Two

The Twelve Steps are baby steps. Step Two says, "We came to believe that a Power greater than ourselves can restore us to sanity." Having admitted that we are powerless, we are prepared to seek and find a source of wisdom and strength outside ourselves. Our inability to do the impossible, to conquer our discontent, to curtail our out-of-control addiction to unhappiness, has driven us to our knees.

Religiously oriented people are reasonably comfortable with the concept of a Higher Power because they already have a measure of faith. But very few individuals take it as a compliment when someone suggests that they are anything less than mentally competent, as implied in the words, "came to believe that a Power greater than ourselves could restore us to sanity." They are offended by the idea that they need to be restored to *sanity.*

Clinically, the word *insanity* denotes mental illness. But that's not what Step Two means by the term. Where addiction and compulsion are concerned, *insanity* is simply repeating the same negative behavior patterns over and over and expecting different results.

Have you ever eaten a huge piece of a gooey dessert when you knew it would make you sick? Have you ever driven your car aware that the gas gauge was on empty? Have you taken an exam you weren't adequately prepared for and then gone to a test ill-prepared again the next week, even though you promised yourself you wouldn't let it happen again? Loosely defined, these behaviors are insane. When Step Two mentions being restored to sanity, it simply means breaking the cycle of self-defeating behavior.

Lauren was the self-reliant daughter of two high achievers. An insightful child, she sensed at an early age that, in order to win her the approval of her parents and other authority figures, she would have to work hard and behave perfectly. In her efforts to please, she lost touch with herself as an individual. Lauren was so busy *performing* that she didn't pay attention to her deeper feelings and needs.

Now, at the age of thirty-six, she feels empty and exhausted. She can't deal with situations she used to be able to handle with ease. Her childhood coping skills of overwork, scrupulosity, and unhealthy self-sacrifice have failed her, but she keeps hurting herself to please others. At this point, she has no option but to admit her powerlessness over her self-destructive behavior, acknowledge the possibility that there is a Power greater than herself, and ask for help.

Step Three

Once an addict is convinced that running his own life under his own power doesn't work and that there *must* be someone out there who can do a better job, he (sometimes reluctantly) chooses to let go and turn his problems over to the God of his understanding. For those individuals who have developed a prior misunderstanding of God rather than a healthy understanding, this can be a challenge.

Fortunately, we don't have to focus obsessively on trying to figure out who God really is in order to correct our misunderstanding. We don't have to strain our finite brains trying to comprehend the nature of the Infinite. We can turn ourselves and our out-of-control habits over to God, even if we don't fully understand, trust, or even like Him. To put this into practice, we simply reach out for help from the people and principles that have been placed before us.

Then we move forward, confident in the knowledge that we will enjoy a spiritual awakening as a result of doing all the steps. This is specifically promised in Step Twelve: "Having had a spiritual awakening as the result of these steps, we continued to practice these principles. . . ." By the time we reach Step Twelve, we will have found a Higher Power with whom we can do business.

Sometimes I think it's harder for lifelong Christians to "let go and let God" than it is for people who are inexperienced in matters of faith. When you've been in the church for so long that you've almost earned patriarchal status, it's tempting to think that you know something and that knowing something gives you a corner on discerning God's will—which, of course, qualifies you to play God. It isn't easy to let go of that delusion and the false sense of security it brings. When we have really surrendered, we cease to fight. No more conniving, calculating, or moving the lights, ballet, and scenery around.

I'm alluding here to a description of compulsive behavior found in AA literature that I find humorous: "Most people try to live by self-propulsion. Each person is like an actor who wants to run the whole show, is forever trying to arrange the lights, the ballet, the scenery, and the players in his own way. If his arrangements would only stay put, if only people would do as he wished, the show would be great. Everyone, including himself, would be pleased."[3] Most people with addictive tendencies can relate to that! Letting go and letting God is a necessity.

Step Four

Step Four reads, "We made a searching and fearless moral inventory of our lives." This step is an exercise in self-awareness. We are encouraged to write down significant attitudes and actions, describe our feelings about them, and identify the character traits from which our attitudes and actions have arisen. Looking honestly at the past—at who we've been and what we've done—helps us understand ourselves better. This self-awareness is the beginning of emotional healing.

Step Four gives us a chance to look beneath our superficial behavior to the place where deeper issues lie. We assess what's actually in our minds and hearts, focus on our own reality, tune in to our feelings, acknowledge our personal agenda, and get honest with ourselves. We expose resentments that have been hiding under the rug, probe the pain and problems we have been holding in secret, and take steps to resolve them. "By discovering what our emotional deformities are, we can move toward their correction," as it says in *Twelve Steps and Twelve Traditions*.[4] This is crucial for misery addicts.

Many people approach this step as if it was a cataloging of their misdeeds. Not so. The fourth step is not intended to be a pointless rehashing of past mistakes. It is not meant to plunge the soul searcher into a cauldron of guilt, shame, or sorrow. It is simply a tool for freeing oneself from old, useless patterns of behavior and finding new ways to live.

The humility to accept our humanity
Step Five

This step asks us to admit to ourselves, to God, and to another human being the exact nature of our wrongs. Such self-revelation leads to self-reconciliation, self-understanding. It's like documenting your bank deposits and expenditures in order to reconcile your monthly bank statement and recognize your current financial status.

There's a saying in recovery circles that people stay as sick as the secrets they keep. Hiding either our assets or our liabilities keeps the spiritual system out of balance. Although the thought of being totally honest with another person can be daunting, the rewards are unquestionable. As one recovering misery addict put it, "It was in applying Step Five to myself and being given the courage to be totally honest with another that I experienced a spiritual transformation. It was an experience of inner healing, a reconciliation with myself, with others, and with a loving God."

In making plans to follow Step Five, we look for a compassionate and noncondemning listener. This helps us relax into our own humanity, maybe for the first time in our lives. We discover that we aren't unusual or different after all. We're fallible but not defective. The listener knows all of our secrets and doesn't think any less of us. She or he doesn't disown or disfellowship us. We are loved and accepted in spite of our human frailties.

Carrie experienced the miracle-working power of this process. An omnicompetent workaholic church administrator, wife, and mother, Carrie was on the verge of total burnout at the age of fifty-one. Her immune system was shot. Her defenses were down. When she was confronted with a troubling family situation, she hit bottom and joined a twelve-step group.

After working through the first four steps and presenting her fifth step to her sponsor, Carrie was amazed at how different she felt: "I never dreamed how universal my experiences would prove to be. I would have never guessed, in admitting the terrible sins I thought made me different from other people and far worse than most, that I would discover how alike we really are. It was a blessed relief to share my history with someone like me. I finally stopped condemning myself."

Carrie experienced the profound benefits of Step Five: her shame was reduced, her backlogged feelings were expressed and expelled, she revealed and relieved her deepest hurts and darkest secrets, and she demolished the barriers she had erected around herself. By dismantling the walls that hid her imperfections, she put an end to her isolation. She is a far more genuine person now. People are drawn to her. She is no longer alone.

Step Six

Carrie's first brush with Step Six—"We were entirely ready to have God remove all these defects of character"—came within days of finishing Step Five. She made a discovery she probably would have missed without the insight into her own character gained from doing Steps Four and Five. Here's what happened.

After a particularly heated meeting of her local church board, Carrie reviewed her conduct as twelve-step literature suggests. She had gotten angry at someone who disagreed with her and argued with him doggedly, invoking the authority of a majority that existed only in her own mind. Looking back at the situation, Carrie saw her behavior for what it was—sheer arrogance. She realized that she was a control freak. For the first time, she loathed her symptoms while continuing to love and respect herself. This demonstrates the value of the first five steps. They motivate people to change while freeing them from self-loathing.

Humbled by her failure, Carrie became entirely willing to have God remove her negative traits of character. En route to the next board meeting, Carrie assured God that she was willing—even eager—to stop controlling. But by the end of the evening, she felt defeated and discouraged. Not only had she failed to control her controlling, but she seemed to have failed more than ever before. In desperation, she telephoned her sponsor.

"Step Six isn't working!" she cried. "Tonight I became willing to have a particular defect of character removed, and then I turned around and did it worse than ever before. I don't understand what happened."

Her sponsor chuckled. "I get more frantic telephone calls in the middle of the night when my sponsorees are on the sixth step than at any other time. Carrie, please read Step Six to me."

"We were entirely ready to have God remove these defects of character," Carrie recited.

"And whose job is it to remove your defects of character?" asked her patient sponsor.

"God's," Carrie replied. After a moment of pensive silence, the insight came. "Aha. As soon as I became willing to have God remove my negative traits, I took control and tried to remove them myself, right?"

"Yes, you rushed into Step Seven before you were ready. Controllers tend to do that because they want immediate results. They try to make 'it' happen. In the agony of failing to change themselves by themselves, they develop the humility needed for Step Seven. Most of us have to fall on our faces in order to develop this kind of humility."

The sponsor went on to explain that Step Six is a fresh reminder of our powerlessness—an opportunity to revisit Step One. We need God's help in the middle of our journey as much as we did at the start. This renewed recognition of powerlessness prepares us for the greater step of faith we are about to take.

Step Seven

At Step Seven, we humbly ask God to remove our shortcomings. At some point in our lives, some problem, some besetting sin, some addiction or compulsion brought us down. Our inflated egos were punctured. We were humiliated. In our pain and shame, we recognized that we couldn't fix what was ailing us. So we asked God to exercise His transforming power on our behalf. We genuinely let go of the reins.

AA literature offers a model for what is known as the Seventh Step Prayer. In this prayer, we ask God to remove every defect of character that stands in the way of our usefulness to Him—not the defects we dislike, not the defects that stand in the way of our popularity, not the defects that make us look stupid or shallow, not the defects that compromise our social standing or reveal our selfish motives—just those that stand in the way of our usefulness to God. This is a very pure, very clear prayer.

Step Eight

There's a reason that Step One comes before Step Two, Step Two comes before Step Three, and so on. Each step rests securely on the foundation of the previous step and prepares us to proceed. Throughout the process, we are incrementally facing the truth about ourselves and our liabilities, while still loving and accepting ourselves. It's a gracious plan.

We have asked God to remove our defects. Little by little, we are being transformed. Our attitudes and actions toward others are changing. Until we have reached this point, we are not even close to being ready to make amends, nor are others ready to receive our amends.

Has anyone ever offered you an apology, only to commit the same offense again five minutes later? His behavior gave the lie to the apology. The amends making was either superficial or motivated by selfishness.

We have to change our attitudes and behaviors before our apologies will be believable. We need to understand what we have done wrong and feel it deeply. We need to know how we have hurt others. After we have taken steps to change our behavior and have shown evidence of that change, our attempts to apologize will be infinitely more meaningful and acceptable.

Amends making is divided into two parts. First, comes Step Eight, "We made a list of people we have harmed and became willing to make amends to them all." This allows us to put aside self-justification and think about the people we have hurt and exactly how we have harmed them. Have we been domineering, inflexible, overprotective, negative, critical, impatient, humorless? We do this step as if there were no ninth step. We don't focus on the amends we will make later. We just concentrate on making the list and becoming willing.[5]

In this process, we are encouraged to face our inappropriate behavior in its subtlest forms. Note this amazing description of negaholism in the *Twelve Steps and Twelve Traditions:* "Suppose that in our family lives we happen to be miserly, irresponsible, callous, or cold. Suppose that we are irritable, critical, impatient. . . . *What happens when we wallow in depression, self-pity oozing from every pore, and inflict that upon those about us?*"[6] Isn't it interesting that negaholism is actually described in AA literature?

The process of self-examination would be intolerably painful were it not for the fact that, by now, our spiritual strength and emotional security have grown to the point that we can face the truth without becoming self-destructive. We are simply making ourselves accountable.

We aren't motivated by the need to gain God's approval or to relieve our own guilt and shame. Apologizing for the sole purpose of freeing ourselves from the burden of guilt would be self-serving. That's not the point at all.

Our real intent in doing Steps Eight and Nine is to heal the bruised and broken relationships of the past, learn the lessons implicit in them, and fit ourselves to be of maximum service to God and humankind. These steps free us to love ourselves and others unconditionally. And in the process of recognizing our need of forgiveness, we become more forgiving of others.

Step Nine

Step Nine reads, "Made direct amends to such people whenever possible, except when to do so would injure them or others." Misery addicts, with all of their gossiping, criticizing, and complaining, can do a great deal of harm. The goal of Step Nine is to make peace with the people we have hurt. Negative attitudes and behaviors from the past have diminished our vitality and robbed us of the joy of living in the present. We want to clear away the wreckage of the past.

Good judgment and careful timing are required in making amends. We must never buy our own peace of mind at the expense of others. For this reason, we're careful to do the first eight steps thoroughly—to face our defects of character and the havoc they have created. Having submitted ourselves to God's transforming power and experienced genuine change, we are prepared to repair and rebuild our relationships. Our words and actions are finally congruent.

Caution is advised when making amends. Just to show how a careless apology can do more harm than good, I share this personal experience. Years ago, a woman apologized to me for having taken an "instant dislike" to me when we met. She had decided that her first impression was wrong, and she felt very guilty. I hadn't realized how she felt until she told me. I was hurt more by her apology than by what had caused it. Frankly, I believe that a confession to God on her part would have been adequate.

Making amends is not synonymous with apologizing. Genuine repentance is about changed behavior. If I say I'm sorry for being late to an appointment, that's an apology. Being prompt for my next appointment is an *amendment*—a change in behavior. If I apologize for keeping you waiting and then continue being tardy, I haven't amended my behavior. The best amends are a changed life.

The genius of living one day at a time
Step Ten

Step Ten is the first of three maintenance steps that bring us into close connection with God and others. It reads, "Continued to take personal inventory and when we were wrong, promptly admitted it." Without this option, we would be at risk for losing our direction and drifting back into old behaviors. Step Ten allows us to clean up our messes as quickly as possible. The other day, my husband spilled grape juice on his dress shirt. I didn't want the stain to dry and become permanent, so I soaked the shirt in boiling water immediately. It's easier to remove a spot while it's fresh, to clean up a spill before it dries, to treat a wound before it festers.

Old Testament scripture offers many examples of people who failed to admit their wrongdoing promptly—Jacob and Esau and Joseph's older brothers being the most notable. These individuals were haunted by unconfessed wrongs, and, as a result, their relationships were painfully compromised. Failing to admit our wrongdoing drives wedges between ourselves and the people we love.

Step Ten has proven to be very valuable to me because it not only enlivens and energizes relationships, it is also an effective antidote to perfectionism. I grew up thinking I had to be flawless. Obviously, there's nothing wrong with wanting to be good, but I was obsessed with perfection. I hadn't come to terms with my fallibility, which meant that I lived a constant state of tension, because I was always trying to avoid making a mistake. Step Ten freed me from that anxious lifestyle. I could stop trying to be perfect and admit that I was human. Rather than striving futilely for some illusory ideal, I knew I could relax, make mistakes, and correct them in a timely way. It's wonderful to be able to admit that I am wrong without having a shame attack.

Thankfully, I no longer live in fear of failure. When I accepted the fact that it was OK to make mistakes, I no longer had to second-guess myself. I no longer had to rationalize and defend every action in order to maintain the illusion of perfection. Whew!

Step Eleven

Step Eleven says, "Sought through prayer and meditation to improve our conscious contact with God as we understand Him, praying only for a knowledge of His will for us and the power to carry that out." Maintaining an ongoing program of recovery is vital, and prayer and meditation are essential to that program. Since communication with God is a personal matter, prayer and meditation may simply be viewed as two of many approaches people can use.

Gail, a newly recovering misery addict, was concerned about how to know when she had established contact with God and how she could be sure God was guiding her. Gail's sponsor described, in her own words, a process of meditation and prayer recommended in AA literature.

Before you go to bed at night, review your day. Ask yourself where you might improve. Ask God's forgiveness for your failings. Ask Him how you can correct your mistakes. Then go to sleep.

When you wake up in the morning, pray and meditate about the day ahead. Remember that prayer is asking for God's help; meditation is listening to His answer. Review your plans for the day, asking that God direct your thinking and keep you from slipping into self-pity, dishonesty, or self-seeking. If you don't know what to do in a given situation, ask God for inspiration. Then relax and take it easy. Don't struggle or worry about your decision—just wait for the answer to come. Meanwhile, calmly do what lies before you.[7]

Gail began to make this her daily practice. The result? She wastes a whole lot less time trying to arrange people and circumstances to suit herself. She no longer manipulates others to get them to do things her way or gets upset when they don't. She is less overwhelmed, anxious, and angry. And she rarely succumbs to self-pity.

Step Twelve

"Having had a spiritual awakening as the result of these steps, we tried to carry this message to alcoholics and to practice these principles in all our affairs." Becoming honest with others and responsible to God helps us to be more authentic. We are genuine, real. Without this, intimacy is impossible.

Step Twelve takes the misery addict beyond the isolating loneliness of addiction and compulsion into a deeper, more meaningful relationship with God and others. We come to love ourselves with a love that comes only from a God-given love of self. A renewed sense of our own value enhances all of our relationships. The *spiritual awakening* promised in Step Twelve is literally the revival of the human spirit, a regaining of vitality, a renewal of our zest for living. We are now fully alive and fully present to God, ourselves, and others.

Hope for Today

The process of internal change begins with a careful examination of who we are, what we do, and how our behavior affects the people around us. We can turn away from our old selves to find a better self. In time, we are transformed by the God of our understanding into the people we were meant to be. Throughout the journey, we practice "experimental religion." We gradually, gently discover who God really is, what He does, and how He relates to us and our problems. The Twelve Steps make the process of change and growth as easy as possible. And the "angels" in our twelve-step groups (sponsors and peers in recovery) are an expression of God's willingness to help us throughout the journey.

Self-Study

1. List five symptoms of misery addiction that you think you have manifested, such as sympathy seeking, martyring, caretaking, acting helpless, etc.
2. For three days, try to control or curtail all these behaviors.
3. If you have found it virtually impossible to abstain, describe to a sponsor or trusted friend one or two instances in which you failed. For example, "I resolved not to caretake people today and discovered that I didn't even realize when I was doing it."
4. Make a list of the undesirable consequences of compulsive caretaking in your own life and the lives of your loved ones, such as "My son says it really annoys him when I hover over him." Describe how the people closest to you are affected by your behavior.

---

1. Alcoholics Anonymous, *Twelve Steps and Twelve Traditions*, 15.

2. Ibid.

3. See Alcoholics Anonymous, *Alcoholics Anonymous: The Story of How Many Thousands of Men and Women Have Recovered from Alcoholism*, 3d ed. (New York: Alcoholics Anonymous World Services, Inc., 1976), 60.

4. Alcoholics Anonymous, *Twelve Steps and Twelve Traditions*, 43.

5. See Alcoholics Anonymous, *Alcoholics Anonymous*, 76–84.

6. Alcoholics Anonymous, *Twelve Steps and Twelve Traditions*, 81. (Italics added.)

7. Alcoholics Anonymous, *Alcoholics Anonymous*, 86, 87.

CHAPTER 14

The Truth Will
Set You Free

Because I remember, I despair. Because I remember,
I have the duty to reject despair.

— Elie Wiesel

We turn now to the broad historical or therapeutic issues that can complicate recovery and compound (enlarge and enrich) the first step. The more dysfunctional or out-of-control your early environment was, the more dysfunctional and out-of-control your present life may be. Even though you may have compensated for the chaos in your early life by creating a lifestyle that is scrupulously controlled and seemingly perfect now, you may very well have unresolved issues.

Regardless of which extreme a person leans toward—being totally out-of-control or overly controlled and controlling—the core issues are the same. These may include shame and self-loathing, immature coping skills, denied or repressed emotions, skewed thoughts and feelings, relationship problems, a tendency to react compulsively in difficult circumstances, and addictive behavior. Please note the historical causes portrayed in the chart that follows:

PAINFUL FAMILY SYSTEMS
(Environments dominated by the "sickest" member)

ALCOHOLIC/ADDICTIVE   WORKAHOLIC/PERFECTIONISTIC
(Dysfunctional system that   (Dysfunctional system that
    looks dysfunctional)   looks functional)

Characterized by: Characterized by:
1. Chaos, unpredictability   1. Stress, tension, rigidity
2. Underprotection   2. Overprotection
3. Physical abandonment   3. Emotional abandonment

←————————— Addiction is a disease of the extreme —————————→

Whether we responded to our childhood dilemma by flipping to one extreme or to the other, we need to realize that we are inclined to over-react or underreact to stress now. Our reactionary style is long-standing and deeply habituated—almost like a reflex. It is appropriate to treat habitual defense mechanisms as addictions. As stated earlier, the same program that works for alcoholics works for people who are struggling with long-standing, deep-seated habits such as raging, manipulation, negativity, perfectionism, and compulsive controlling.

For people dealing with the kinds of issues implied in the chart above, Step One becomes broad and comprehensive. It includes many relation-ship habits. As my self-awareness grows, I become increasingly aware of my knee-jerk reactions to people and circumstances and the cognitive and/or emotive filter system that drives them—usually in the wrong di-rection. Perhaps you too have caught yourself regressing to childish be-havior at the worst possible moment and then wondering what "pos-sessed" you. That's what I'm talking about.

In my case, because I was a child of a workaholic and perfectionistic family system, my reference point for normal was skewed! I adapted to unhealthy circumstances in ways that worked for me back then, but the coping skills that worked so well in childhood turned against me in adult-hood. In adulthood, peers did not respond as well to my dysfunctional behaviors as had my parents and teachers! But by then the habits were so deeply embedded that I couldn't quit. I couldn't even see that they weren't working anymore.

My first step had to include all of these deeply habituated behaviors: caretaking, control, workaholism, perfectionism, people pleasing, religious addiction, and relationship addiction. The step grew larger and larger as my awareness grew. It became increasingly inclusive. I stopped trying to fight so many battles on so many fronts and enlisted help. I had to admit the obvious: I couldn't do it single-handedly; I couldn't gain the victory no matter how hard I tried. This didn't make me bad. It just meant that I was powerless in the face of such overwhelming odds. Surrendering to this fact brought relief and paved the way to greater and greater calmness and peace of mind. Voilà! The antithesis of misery addiction!

The truth versus *your* truth

Your experience as a three-year-old, your reality as a five-year-old, your perceptions as an eleven-year-old, your perspective as a seventeen-year-old, and everywhere else in between—this constitutes your reality, unadulterated by other people's explanations, excuses, alibis, etc. Denying your truth is pointless, as you will see.

That which determined your reactions when you were a child, that which colored your present worldview, and that which triggers your reactions in the here and now is your sense of what happened in the then and there. These experiences are hardwired into your brain. They color your present reality.

Repressed emotions locked deep inside are the byproducts of old perspectives, and they create a screen or filter through which everything that happens now has to pass. Even if your old perceptions were inaccurate or skewed, they affected your worldview and created feelings that remain locked within you. To dispute them cognitively will not necessarily remove the residual feelings. As one of my advisors said, "The amygdala [a clump of neurons deep in the brain that regulate the flight or fight mechanism] doesn't understand English."

There's no point in trying to rationalize, wish, or pray your reality away. That's probably what you have been trying to do for years—telling yourself that you're imagining things, that your pain isn't important, that everything that went wrong in your family is your fault, etc. That approach doesn't work. You can't minimize trauma or deny it, you can't excuse abusive behavior that has been perpetrated against you, and you can't assign blame to yourself as a child and still hope for health and healing as an adult. Today, you must "believe the child" and honor his or her emotions in order to enjoy long-lasting relief from the pain of the past.

Please note this statement by Dr. Alice Miller, internationally known expert on the impact of child abuse and neglect: "It's not the traumas people experience in childhood that make them sick. It's the inability to express the trauma."[1]

Finding a safe place to express your feelings is vital to recovery. Dr. Miller suggests that people need to unburden themselves of old pain. This provides an opportunity for doctors, nurses, counselors, pastors, and other helping professionals to be of service.[2] I'm not sure we can serve suffering people as Dr. Miller suggests until we have addressed the healing of our own wounds. Do we want to be wounded healers or unhealed wounders? The point is that a therapeutic experience is required.

Facing the truth

To discover your personal truth, begin by asking yourself, "What was it like for me growing up?" And then invite the infant, toddler, preadolescent, or adolescent within you to speak. Don't argue with her, don't deny her the right to her own reality, don't try to explain her perceptions away. Respect the fact that what you experienced is your truth. You have a right to feel your feelings, and you have the right to tell someone about them.

You may wish to write your memories in a journal. You will benefit from sharing your story in group or individual therapy or talking about it privately with a twelve-step sponsor. Don't overthink historical events. Feel them. Grieve them. Be angry. Honor your own reality. Show compassion to the child you once were for the undue suffering you faced in childhood and its residual effects in adulthood. Remember, there is a vast difference between feeling *sorrow* for yourself and feeling *sorry* for yourself. In this context, sorrow is good. We need to grieve our losses—even the loss of normalcy.

I encourage you not to do this kind of cathartic work in isolation. Find safe people and safe places where you will have the support you need for a process that can be, at times, painful and challenging. In the end, it is very rewarding and very liberating.

Blame versus accountability

Prior to hitting bottom in my clean addictions and going through inpatient treatment, I thought that the truth which set people free was doctrinal or theological in nature—the truth about God or deity. Today I believe it's more than that. I am convinced that we have to face the truth about ourselves: our history; our learned, self-defeating behaviors; our understanding and misunderstanding of God; and our true potential as creatures of God's creative and restorative power. It is this truth that sets us free.

Some people—Christians especially—hesitate to open the doors of their minds and hearts to truth at this level. They are hesitant to examine the past. There are reasons for their reluctance. It may be based on fear, either the fear of what they will find or the fear that they won't be able to handle what they find. Some are even afraid that God won't be able to handle what they discover and that He will somehow be annoyed by their very attempt to uncover hidden truth, past abuse, etc.

Others assume that exploring the past is equivalent to dishonoring or disrespecting their parents. They think that making parents accountable for their misdeeds would be a violation of the fifth commandment. Mind you, confronting a person's behavior is not the same as dishonoring the person. Despising the sin is not synonymous with hating the sinner. At some point, children who have grown up in abusive, addictive environments deserve to be heard, honored, and respected. They have a right to share their truth.

Many people believe that because we can't change the events of the past there is no point in talking about them. Wrong. A brief examination of past events—not just talking about them but allowing ourselves to feel and express the pain, fear, and anger—can bring considerable relief. As a result, we may begin to notice relationship patterns in our present life that reflect old abuses, old trust issues, and old fears. Our historical issues affect our present reactions and relationships. We may see that we're taking out our repressed anger on people who don't deserve it. We may be afraid of people now who remind us of former perpetrators. Recognizing this can guide us in determining the areas of our lives that we need to address therapeutically.

Will therapy compromise my faith?

When I went into codependency treatment in 1986, I admitted myself to a hospital-based program that had no religious affiliation. I was afraid that I would lose my faith, but God was bigger than my worst fears. When I walked in the door, I spied a sign on the wall that said "Who the #%*& do you think you are?" That put me in a tizzy. *What's a nice Christian lady like me doing in a place like this?* I thought. But I was too beaten down, too depressed to run.

I soon discovered that God was far greater than superficial things such as wall plaques. I witnessed miracles. I *experienced* miraculous healing. The God of my understanding was more concerned about me and the other patients in the program coming out of death alive than He was about the wall decor or the vocabulary or religious affiliation of the counselors.

Today I know that God wanted me and the other patients to have life and have it more abundantly. God was not limited by human frailty and fallibility. It is this awareness that has allowed me to work as a professional in the field of addiction and recovery for thirty-three years. God uses me in spite of, and sometimes *because of,* my imperfections.

I see more miracles in that treatment setting every week than most people see in the church setting their whole lives. I'm not casting aspersions on my beloved church or any other church when I say this. My point is that God is more open-minded than most people think. I believe that God works best with people whose problems have driven them to their knees. He has many ways to accomplish the miracle of healing. People who have been driven to their knees by their addictions or the addictions of a loved one have a level of humility and willingness that makes them eager to go to whatever lengths are necessary to recover. That kind of willingness provides a ready backdrop for miracles of the highest order.

Powerlessness doesn't mean *helplessness*

Hopeless thinking and helpless behavior fuel misery addiction. Negaholics think their problems are worse than anyone else's. They believe they are beyond help. In reality, they aren't as hopeless and helpless as they think. But they certainly are powerless over their negative way of thinking. They have yet to discover that powerlessness is empowering.

Have you ever tried to move an object that is too heavy for you—like a railroad tie or a grand piano? Long-standing, deep-seated habits are like a grand piano. There is no way I could move a grand piano single-handedly. Granted, I might be able to nudge it an inch or two, but I couldn't possibly move it to the next room—never mind across town. Does that make me weak or helpless? No, I'm just not a piano mover.

Do you think that if I flexed my muscles, if I wanted to move the piano badly enough, or if I lifted weights for a few days, *then* I could bench-press a piano? What if I read the Bible more, prayed harder, or exercised my willpower better? Could I juggle grand pianos then? Hardly! Suppose I went back to the top of the list and started again. Would I succeed? No. Regardless of how often or how hard I tried, I could only fail because the task is impossible.

Not until I recognize the futility of my efforts, accept the sheer impossibility of moving grand pianos single-handedly, and get some help, will I succeed at getting the piano moved. Admitting that we can't do the impossible, and asking for help doesn't mean we're weak or bad. It just means we don't have the strength and skill to do it alone.

At one point in my life, I found myself in the grip of first one and then another ill-gotten habit of thinking, feeling, and behaving. These habits were so deep-seated that I was powerless to change them, no matter how badly I wanted to or how hard I tried. I knew it was crazy to keep repeating my self-destructive behavior, but I couldn't seem to gain the victory on the basis of willpower alone. Because I thought I *should* be able to conquer my habits, I tried extremely hard to do so. When that didn't work, I tried harder still. Even after I realized that I was beating my head against a brick wall, I didn't quit—I just kept pounding.

Not until I acknowledged my powerlessness and turned to a reputable "moving company" that had been in business since 1935 did I succeed in getting the piano moved. By calling them and asking for help, I surrendered my problem to their superior strength and expertise. *My* strength was thus made perfect in weakness. I guess I'm in pretty good company because the apostle Paul talked about God's strength being made perfect in human weakness too.[3] Powerlessness is extremely empowering. It puts us in touch with a Source of wisdom and strength that can do for us what we cannot do for ourselves. I can live with that.

Addiction is the human condition

By its very nature, that which most believers call *sin* is addictive. Addiction is the human condition. The goal of recovery is not freedom from the chronic disease we call "addiction." The goal of recovery is not sinlessness. It's awareness—the kind of awareness that leads to humility and teachability and a recognition of our need for God's goodness and righteousness. We're already OK. We've already been taken care of. What else can I say?

Victim no more

Hang on to your hat. This section is going to be a taste of freedom— a preview of what is to come if you get therapy and work the Twelve Steps. To introduce this subject, I have to show you something that comes straight out of the *Big Book* of Alcoholics Anonymous. It's found in the context of Step Four, which reads, "We made a searching and fearless moral inventory of ourselves."

After giving a simple outline of how to do Step Four, the *Big Book* offers one of the best insights I've ever come across: "We went back through our lives. Nothing counted but thoroughness and honesty. When we were finished, we considered it carefully. The first thing apparent was that this world and its people were often quite wrong." Well, *amen* to that! That's the problem for us misery addicts: we can't get people to act right, and we can't be happy if they don't.

"To conclude that others were wrong was as far as most of us ever got. The usual outcome was that people continued to wrong us, and we stayed sore." The passage continues, "We turned back to the list, for it held the key to the future. We were prepared to look at it from an entirely different angle. We began to see that the world and its people really dominated us. In that state, the wrong-doing of others, fancied or real, had power to actually kill."[4]

Let's talk about the word *dominated* for a minute. To be dominated is to be controlled by another, to give someone or something the power to determine our mood and our self-esteem. It is to give them the power of life or death over you.

Now I'm going to insert a phrase from the first paragraph I quoted into the middle of the second paragraph I quoted. Watch this: "We began to see that the world and its ["often quite wrong"] people really dominated us." Now, close your eyes and repeat that phrase: "We began to see that the world and its 'often quite wrong' people really dominated us." What that tells me is that we martyrs or victims give the world and its "often quite wrong" people the power of life or death over us. If that's true, then whose problem is it? I rest my case.

Note the long-term implications of this. We can break the habit of letting the world and its "often quite wrong" people dominate us! Misery addicts are dominated by the world and its "often quite wrong" people. We don't have to continue doing that. If we use the tools available, we can recover.

Firing false gods

From the people in our early lives who assumed the position of God—parents, authority figures, and anyone who rightly or wrongly took control of our bodies and spirits—we created a concept or picture of God. God took on their personalities, their traits of character. Few adults sense on a conscious level how much these archaic pictures of God have affected their ability to relate to a loving and trustworthy Higher Power in the present.

And few realize how addicted they are to their misunderstandings of God, how dependent they are on those false images. Many Christians are held hostage by an abusive conscience. They have bonded with a harsh, judgmental God in the same way human hostages often bond with and become addicted to their abusers. This is known as the Stockholm syndrome, after a case in which a group of people, who were held as prisoners for a long period of time in Stockholm, Sweden, defended their captors after being released. By some accounts, one woman hostage ended up marrying one of her captors. Persisting in victimizing ourselves to an abusive environment (family, church, God) is martyring.

Many misery addicts have made God into a cruel taskmaster—a God who can't be pleased and will not be appeased. For those of us who have done this, stepping out of the victim role requires being willing to reframe our concept of God. Freeing ourselves from bondage to our idols, our false images of God, is a necessary but frightening part of the developmental process. The more security one has found in his or her false picture of God, the more unnerving it will be to let it go. But it is possible.

When I was in this phase of my recovery, I was terrified. I stepped off one curb and found myself in the middle of six lanes of swirling traffic. I had the panic attack of all panic attacks. How could I survive until I reached the other curb—the point of being comfortable with the God of my new understanding?

In this state, I found hope and comfort in the promise of Step Twelve—that the result of doing the first eleven steps is a spiritual awakening. For a brief period of time, that's all I had to hang on to. I placed my faith in that promise, and it got me through. I did enjoy a spiritual awakening.

Trusting the God you don't understand

When I realized that my understanding of God was, in fact, a major *misunderstanding,* my first impulse was to rush out and buy six new translations of the Bible and a set of Bible commentaries and study them nonstop until I got my misunderstanding corrected. I was afraid that if I didn't get it figured out by sundown, I would die before I awoke. Isn't that just like an immature addict?

If ever in my life I have heard God's voice, I heard it then. I knew for a certainty that if I obeyed the impulse to take control of the situation and try to solve it overnight, I would be "using"—acting out my disease. I had to jump off the cliff, go into a free fall, and trust the process—which is exactly what I did. I've never regretted that moment.

My plan to study my way to a correct understand of God was bound to fail, because my spiritual problem was not cognitive. I had an undergraduate degree in religion from Andrews University by then. I knew quite a bit about God. The problem was in my heart, my unconscious, my soul. The healing I needed was emotional, spiritual. And it came about as a natural result of working the Twelve Steps.

Incidentally, I had to go back to about the age of five to find a friendly, loving, compassionate God—back to the days when I used to sing in Sabbath School, "Rock, rock, rock, little boat on the sparkling sea." That's where I found God. I'm confident that wherever *you* go to find your Higher Power and however long the journey takes, God will be there.

Having had a spiritual awakening . . .

Today, I'm grateful to say that I can't define God. I don't understand God. But I believe in and trust Him. I'm comfortable with AA's notion that every individual has the right to define God for himself or herself. Nobody that you sit with in the church pew on Sabbath or Sunday morning has exactly the same concept of God that you do anyway. God isn't limited by our perceptions. If God were definable, we'd all be in trouble.

Back to the promise from the *Twelve Steps and Twelve Traditions* that got me through the early phases of my spiritual journey:

> So, practicing these Steps, we had a spiritual awakening about which finally there was no question. Looking at those who were only beginning and still doubted themselves, the rest of us were able to see the change setting in.
>
> From great numbers of such experiences, we could predict that the doubter who still claimed that he hadn't gotten the "spiritual angle" . . . would presently love God and call Him by name.[5]

God has it covered. We don't have to worry about ourselves or anyone we love. No matter our past experiences or present struggles, we will enjoy a spiritual awakening as a result of working these steps.

Hope for Today

Here's a personal testimony from a woman who was programmed to negativity from her very birth. Since getting sober in AA several years ago, she has struggled heroically to arrest her addiction to misery. "When I first came into AA, I hated God and all that He stood for. Religious terminology made the hair on the back of my neck stand up. I couldn't believe that God loved or cared for me. But as I worked the steps in AA, my understanding of God grew. My God today is the loving God I needed all along. Now I'm using the same steps that helped me stop drinking to find freedom from negaholism. It hurts as much to see how much harm my negaholism did as it hurt to see how much harm my drinking did. But I know that God can remove my defects of character. I'm not yet the person I want to be but, thank God, I'm not the person I used to be. I trust God to change me one day at a time."—*Nancy G.*

Self-Study

1. Did you have an experience at home, school, or church as a child that left you feeling ashamed or inadequate? Write a paragraph about it.
2. Do you recall making an innocent mistake and being humiliated by an authority figure when you were young? Imagine that person coming to you now and telling you that they were wrong. How would you feel?
3. Find a photograph of yourself as a youngster. Playing the part of a kind parent or gentle guardian, write a sympathetic statement to that child absolving him or her of blame for behaving like a child. Acknowledge that it's OK to make mistakes and remind yourself that you are valuable and lovable just the way you are.
4. Invite the God of your understanding to guide you in finding appropriate therapeutic help to lead you in the process of healing.

---

1. Alice Miller, *Thou Shalt Not Be Aware* (New York: Farrar, Straus, and Giroux, 1984), vii.
2. Ibid.
3. See 2 Corinthians 12:9.
4. Alcoholics Anonymous, *Alcoholics Anonymous,* 65, 66.
5. Alcoholics Anonymous, *Twelve Steps and Twelve Traditions,* 109.

CHAPTER 15

Where the Rubber Meets the Road

A woman will always sacrifice herself if you give her the opportunity.
It is her favorite form of self-indulgence.

— W. Somerset Maugham

As we have seen, people's vulnerability to addictive substances and activities is influenced by both heredity and environment. We used to think that such vulnerability was created by a family history of addiction and abuse, but we have broadened our understanding to include any kind of preoccupation and drivenness—not just flagrant addiction and abuse.

Today we know that people are not predisposed to dependency disorders by familial alcoholism, drug addiction, overwork, or the modeling of victim and martyr behavior per se. Their vulnerability arises from living in an atmosphere of high stress and low nurturing. Those variables are consistent. A high-stress, low-nurturing environment leaves the adult child spiritually empty, socially insecure, and emotionally needy.

Positive intentions and negative results

Nurturing is more that affection. Nurturing involves celebrating a child—rejoicing in his existence, honoring her uniqueness, focusing on and supporting his development! Nurturing adults provide gentle guidance and encouragement. Parents who work, play, and worship moderately are readily able to do this. Parents who work, play, or worship obsessively are limited in their ability to do so. If they are obsessed with legalism or perfectionism, they are at risk for viewing their children as projects instead of people. I found it very painful to admit, while working on my fourth and fifth steps, that I had objectified my own children in this way.

Many children reared in religious homes who have been required to memorize and recite their memory verses every Sabbath or Sunday since they were two years old end up spiritually bankrupt. Many children who have attended parochial schools their whole lives and whose command of Bible doctrines and church standards is impeccable still end up spiritually starved.

Spiritual emptiness isn't about church or no church; it's about high stress and low nurturing. Write it in the sky—high stress and low nurturing. And it can happen in churchaholic families as well as alcoholic families.

Children reared in legalistic environments often experience God differently than their parents and pastors try to present Him. In an earlier book I pointed out that when we think we're teaching kids to love and trust God, they may be learning to doubt Him. When we think we're teaching them to appreciate Jesus' death on the cross, they may be developing a distaste for everything the cross represents. When we think we're teaching them to look forward to eternity, they may be learning to overlook the beauty of the moment. When we think we're teaching them high ideals, they may be learning low self-worth and fear of failure.[1]

Children who come out of ultra-conservative systems may view God as critical and condemning, unfriendly and unapproachable. At the same time, they may dislike themselves and doubt their abilities. They may have a negative concept of themselves, a sense of worthlessness, a damaged will, and a broken spirit.

By contrast, healthy families produce children with strong, positive identities and a sense of personal worth. They have a friendly, affirming God. These children maintain an intact will and an enlivened spirit. Think of the difference between a spirited animal and a dispirited one, and you will see my point. Spirited creatures are full of curiosity, energy, enthusiasm, and passion. Dispirited creatures are listless, lifeless.

CONSEQUENCES OF EARLY SPIRITUAL EXPERIENCE	
Healthy Family System	Addictive or Obsessive System
Gentle, friendly God/parents Healthy identity (self-confidence) Intact will (power of choice) Enlivened spirit	Harsh Higher Power/parents Negative view of self (self-doubt) Damaged will Broken spirit

If a child's will is broken and his spirit crushed in a strict, austere, disapproving environment, he is likely to distrust God and dislike himself. As a result, he may have trouble forming close connections with anyone—human or divine. In addictive environments, a child "doesn't just develop low self-esteem. He develops no self. And then some well-meaning Christian comes along and warns him that his greatest battle is going to be with self. The battle is not with self. It's with *lack* of self!"[2]

Knowing this helps me to appreciate the complexity of the healing process and the time it takes to mature emotionally and spiritually. Identity development and sanctification are about growing up emotionally and spiritually, in that order. This takes time. The concept of sanctification as the work of a lifetime was vague to me until I understood the Twelve Steps as a means of achieving emotional and spiritual growth.

The antidote to our spiritual problem—our inability to love the Lord with all our hearts and our neighbor as ourselves—is simple. If a high-stress, low-nurturing environment has compromised our ability to develop a healthy relationship with ourselves and our Higher Power, then we must create a low-stress, high-nurturing lifestyle in order to pick up the stitches that were dropped when our characters were "knitted." Even our church affiliations need to fit the low-stress and high-nurturing model.

Recovery needs to be as easy as possible. The least stressful way I know to regain our strength, revive our spirits, and reestablish a healthy sense of self is to use the Twelve Steps. How simple is that? Simple? Yes. Easy? No.

A variation on the golden rule

Here's a novel idea that I think is based on good psychology and good religion. If being able to live the "great commandment" is important, if what the Bible says about loving others as we love ourselves is true,[3] then somewhere along the way it is legitimate for us to do whatever is necessary to learn to experience our own preciousness on a deep internal level.

Have you ever tried to muster self-love and self-respect? It's virtually impossible. That's because most of us put the cart before the horse. Self-love is the effect—not the cause—of healthy self-care. We don't practice healthy self-care because we consider it selfish.

Most children of alcoholics learn early in life that they have to take care of everyone but themselves. Even children in religiously addicted or legalistic environments get it backwards. They, too, learn that self-care is wrong, inappropriate. Both grow up with the "don't be selfish" injunction ringing in their ears.

We need to put first things first. We need to learn how to practice healthy self-care which will lead to the ability to experience our preciousness. In reality, taking care of ourselves is not an act of selfishness or self-centeredness. It's what healthy, mature people do. We are supposed to love and care for ourselves and respect and protect the gifts God has given us.

People who, as children, were compelled to deny their normal needs and deprive themselves unduly in order to serve others have to view the golden rule as a two-sided coin. First, we must treat ourselves with as much love and respect as we would recommend that a dear friend use to love and care for himself or herself. Once we have learned to do that, we will be free to love others with a love that comes only from a God-given love of self. Then we will be able to practice the golden rule from a position of abundance rather than codependence—from a place of maturity and mental health rather than a place of insatiable neediness and neurotic insecurity.

The toughest decision you'll ever make

The decision I'm about to suggest is hard for misery addicts because it flies in the face of the deeply embedded beliefs described above. Next to our Christian commitment, the most important and most difficult decision we will ever make is that of making our own well-being our highest priority.

Nonsense, you say? The Bible says that we must love and care for ourselves before we can love and care for our neighbors. End of story. It's our Christian duty to love and care for ourselves and treat ourselves with respect. In many cases, this is something we were never taught nor was it modeled to us. In some cases the opposite may have been preached from the pulpit.

Having learned to sacrifice ourselves in childhood, we're operating out of an emotional deficit now. We're giving generously to others when our own bank account is overdrawn—writing checks that will come back marked "insufficient funds." Before we can afford to give, we have to build up our own reserves. This is not an act of selfishness. At the end of the day, it is the very thing that makes genuine selflessness possible.

Permission to do less

When I was in treatment, my therapist gave me permission to do less. "Carol, you need to cut yourself some slack." That sounded good, but I didn't know how. Here are a few behavioral changes that worked for me: Cut your to-do list in half. Or shred it entirely. Eliminate. Delegate. Let someone else do it. Do it later, or don't do it at all. Remind yourself that God doesn't need your help. Resist the compulsion to grab the football and run with it. Let someone else make the touchdown. Or let them fumble the ball. It doesn't matter. Give yourself a break.

In order to recover, we have to give ourselves permission to make changes! We can't live with our adrenaline systems operating in hyperdrive all the time. Adrenaline is high-octane energy. We need plenty of downtime to recuperate.

Permission to slow down

Do you happen to have a competitive spirit? Or am I the only person on the planet who calculates time and distance when I'm traveling to make sure that I arrive at my destination in less time than it took the last time? Now that I'm in recovery, I've stopped trying to figure out how many miles over the speed limit I can go and get away with it. I've stopped scanning the horizon constantly for speed traps. Now I go three miles *under* the speed limit. Maybe this is sanctification by senility (or the high price of gasoline).

Most martyrs pride themselves on doing more, better, faster. No more! That symptom has got to go! We have to take a chill pill, cool our jets, stop racing around like idiots. Life isn't a contest. God is in charge of our temporal and eternal welfare and the temporal and eternal welfare of the people we love. He doesn't need our help. Have you ever read God's promise, "before they call, I will answer" (Isaiah 65:24, KJV)?

Permission to resign

Dr. Archibald Hart, professor of psychology at Fuller Theological Seminary and author of several books on overcoming tension and stress, asserts that Christians are exceptionally prone to hyperactivity because of the pressure to be good. "We are . . . ignorant about how the pressure we feel trying to live good lives can cause severe anxiety problems. Being good by relying on our own resources is a lost cause. The harder we try in our own strength, the more our lives become stressful. That is not what God wants from us."[4]

In order to live a low-stress, high-nurturing lifestyle, you may have to resign from a few boards, committees, church leadership roles, task forces, optional duties at work, and volunteer activities. Pare it down to one thing. Sit on *one* committee or board but don't chair it. You will be pleased to discover that you aren't indispensable. The world will continue to revolve.

Dr. Hart recommends paying close attention to our stress tolerance. Once we learn to recognize when we are getting overwhelmed, we need to set boundaries and do everything in our power not to exceed them. We need to set limits and tell everyone, even our loved ones, to back off if they try to push us past our limits.[5]

Recently, I had an unfortunate experience that resulted from failing to heed this advice. For years, I made it a personal policy not to accept more than one outside speaking appointment per quarter. And then, due to the urging of several people, I compromised my boundaries and accepted four major appointments almost back-to-back. I'm 100 percent certain that my ego played a big part in this. I can't blame anyone else. I exceeded my own boundaries. The result was a transient ischemic attack, a mild stroke, from which I have now fully recovered. But it was a wake-up call—one that I take very seriously.

Permission to stop striving

Being the compulsive overachiever that I am, I was thoroughly impressed—even inspired—by a friend who confessed that when she enrolled in her doctoral program, she promised herself she would invest a minimum amount of effort. She was determined to abstain from over-driven striving. She had nothing to prove. She wasn't competing with anyone for prestige or position. She didn't have to kill herself to get the top A in the class. She learned the material, did what was required, and got average grades. Imagine that!

Permission to ask for help

One of the best things we can do to reduce stress and unhappiness in our lives is to stop trying to bear our burdens alone. We need to let others help us. Humbling ourselves and asking for help is not a skill that comes easily for codependent victims and martyrs who have been schooled in the do-it-yourself way of thinking, but it can be done.

Many children of alcoholics, addicts, and workaholics learned when they were young that they were on their own. Because no one was available to guide them or protect them, they became antidependent. Now they find it hard to ask for help. They don't want to bother anyone with their petty problems, and they don't want to be obligated to anyone. They don't want to place their trust in others or give away their power—let anybody else control them.

In reality, asking for help does not equate giving away our power, because, as long as we do the asking, we're still in charge of the situation. We're owning our own prerogatives and maintaining control of our own destiny. Asking for help isn't the same as giving away our power. Here's an example. Hal, a dear friend, learned the importance of asking for help when he was more than sixty years old. Hal was doing some landscaping that required moving heavy timbers around on a hillside. Naturally, he tried to do it all by himself. At one point, he tripped while carrying a log and tumbled downhill, rolling over and over until he landed under the log, so battered and bruised that he couldn't move. Ouch!

When we have a problem or a project that's too big for us, it's OK to ask for help. I don't know about you, but my parents forgot to teach me that. Now, I make it a practice to ask for help several times every day—even if I think I don't need it. Asking for help is a good habit to get into because it keeps us grounded and humble.

Permission to rest and relax

Medical experts say that stress activates a hormone (cortisol) that interferes with the brain's ability to process natural tranquilizers that increase good feelings. Serotonin is the neurotransmitter that enhances the brain's ability to feel positive and good. Cortisol blocks this natural tranquilizer from reaching its receptor sites. The inevitable result is pessimism, negativity, anxiety, and depression.

Behaviors that reduce or diminish our natural tranquilizers include stress, excitement, conflict, hurriedness, under-assertiveness, lack of sleep, lack of adequate rest and relaxation, poor dietary practices, use of caffeine, and the compulsion to control or manage the universe. Where have we heard that before?

Dr. Archibald Hart suggests that "the realization that a reduced level of stress will restore your natural tranquilizers unlocks the key to recovery. . . . You have to take responsibility for lowering your stress level in order to cure your anxiety."[6] Repeat after me: we have to take responsibility for lowering our stress level in order to cure our anxiety.

Hart describes stress in three simple ways: Stress is being stretched beyond our limits. Stress is overextending ourselves without adequate time for recovery. And stress is believing we can do more than our human frame can take.[7] I don't know about you, but I've indulged in every one of those delusional activities.

Dr. Hart gives a plug for accepting our powerlessness when he says that many Christians are ignorant about how the pressures they feel from trying to live good lives can cause severe anxiety problems. "Being good by relying on your own resources is a lost cause," he adds.[8]

One of my favorite Bible verses is Psalm 121:4, "He never slumbers or sleeps but watches over His people day and night"(*The Clear Word*). Knowing that there is a Power greater than myself who never slumbers or sleeps helps me to let go of my worries and take time to rest and relax.

Annie, a brilliant woman, was a master teacher by profession. She appeared on my doorstep while her son was in treatment for chemical dependence. The primary care facility where he was being treated recommended that she come to The Bridge to address her codependency issues before her son came home.

In the process of doing her first step, Annie acknowledged that she was as much an addict as her son—she was a workaholic, perfectionist, and compulsive caretaker. This combination of addictions had led her to martyr herself to the point of ruining her health, neglecting her children, and losing her family. But she had been named "Teacher of the Year" in the school system where she worked—twice. Annie's willingness to face her addictions and codependencies and develop a twelve-step program of her own was a tremendous source of inspiration and encouragement to her son in his recovery. She was a woman of great faith, and on that basis, she was ready and willing to relax and entrust herself and her son to God.

Permission to establish and maintain boundaries

Most negaholics hand their personal power to others. Fear of rejection or disapproval leads them to let other people control them. This habit can be very deep-seated. Codependency treatment may be required in order to break free of the victim mentality. Good treatment programs include skill training in boundary setting. Many experts agree that self-empowerment is the key to achieving tranquility and surviving the long-term ravages of anxiety.

Permission to end conflict

Next to stress, conflict is the most common destroyer of our natural tranquilizers. It triggers the fight-or-flight mechanism that sets off the overproduction of adrenaline. Chronic, ongoing conflict can be extremely damaging to body and soul. "You must either find a solution that gets rid of the conflict or move yourself out of the conflict situation," says Dr. Hart.[9]

Most people have unresolved conflicts, personality clashes, and philosophical differences with others. When you have tried every means at your disposal to mediate a conflict, and nothing has worked, it's OK to stop power struggling and face the fact that the problem can't be fixed. It's OK to remove yourself from the situation or remove the situation from yourself. Don't batter your brain or body against a brick wall too long. Be kind to yourself. It's OK to turn your back and walk away from situations that defy resolution.

One would hope that this doesn't become a frequent event. Certainly, if a pattern of repeated personal conflict emerges in our lives, we need to be willing to look at what we're doing that contributes to the repetitious cycle. The fourth step is a marvelous tool for developing self-awareness and taking responsibility for our part in relationship problems. But even this may not resolve every conflict, because a relationship can only be as healthy as each party is willing and able to make it. It's OK to accept defeat. It's part of life.

Permission to resign from the Trinity

Knowing how important it is that we lower our stress and thus enhance the proper functioning of our bodies' natural tranquilizers, we really have no option but to resign from the Trinity and let the God of our understanding do what He does best. For people who are trapped in the spin cycle of worry and anxiety, letting go and letting God can be a huge relief. But many martyrs are unable to let go, because the practice of managing our own lives and everyone else's is so deeply habituated. We'd be bored if we didn't have to manage the entire universe.

People who want to stop playing God but haven't been able to let go can find help at Al-Anon. Al-Anon addresses the habit of compulsive controlling and micromanaging. It is kindergarten for healthy detachment.

If you've been playing God, if you've been trying to be someone else's savior, and you simply cannot stop, run—don't walk—to the nearest Al-Anon. Al-Anon can be a great blessing to anyone who is caught in an obsessive pattern of caretaking, controlling, worrying, and martyring. My prescription for such individuals is "Al-Anon for Life." It will help you deal with out-of-control people and circumstances. Best of all, it will help you focus on your own sobriety, serenity, and salvation and not on everyone else's.

God really doesn't need our help.

Hope for Today

When I was sitting in a hospital-based treatment facility after my first bout with anxiety and depression twenty-two years ago, I met a woman who taught me a valuable lesson. I'm sure she had no idea what she had done. She was not a counselor; she was one of my fellow patients. One day, she purported to have the answer to a casual question posed by another patient. As soon as the glib answer popped out of her mouth, she stopped herself, put her hand over her mouth, and said, "Wait a minute. I am not an oracle." Her example of instant humility has been an untold blessing to me. It gave me permission to stop trying to be all-knowing and all-powerful—something I was not constitutionally capable of anyway. "I am not an oracle" has become my mantra.

Self-Study

1. If you were reared in a fundamentalist environment, did you develop a positive view of self and of a friendly, affirming God? Or did you develop a negative view of self and of a stern, disapproving God? Are you willing to address these issues if need be?
2. Ask yourself what you can do now to create an environment of low stress and high nurturing for yourself and your family.
3. Make a list of all of your extracurricular committees and responsibilities. Which of them would you be willing to give up?
4. In order to begin establishing boundaries, practice saying No in inconsequential situations such as refusing the bite-sized food sample offered at the supermarket. Begin working up the cour-

age to say No the next time someone asks you to do him a favor or tries to badger you into volunteering for something you don't want to do.

5. As you make these behavioral changes, share your feelings and struggles with a sponsor or mentor. Celebrate your victories.

---

1. See Carol Cannon, *Never Good Enough,* 24.

2. Ibid., 7.

3. See Matthew 19:19.

4. Archibald Hart, *The Anxiety Cure* (Nashville, Tenn.: Word Publishing, 1999), 13.

5. Ibid., 22.

6. Ibid., 31.

7. Ibid., 141.

8. Ibid., 13.

9. Hart, *The Anxiety Cure,* 97, 98.

CHAPTER 16

And When We Have Come to Ourselves

When he finally came to his senses, he said . . . "I will go home
to my father. . . ." [And the father said], "[T]his son of mine was
dead and has returned to life. . . ." So the party began.
— Luke 15: 17, 18, 24, TLB

My name is Carol, and I'm a recovering misery addict, workaholic, perfectionist, caretaker, controller, all purpose overdoer of everything. The other day I found myself stretched out in the parking lot of my son and daughter-in-law's condominium in Jamaica Plain, Massachusetts, halfway under a parked car, reaching to get the Frisbee my grandson had just thrown. My khakis were filthy, my arms were tired, and I was feeling pure, unadulterated gratitude and joy. I was home at last, and it took me only sixty-five years to get there. That is where the steps take us—all twelve of them. To quote Martin Luther King Jr., "Thank God Almighty, I'm free at last!"

Occupying my body

I've concluded that I'm a slow learner—and that's OK. I was a fast learner at the age of eight—way too fast. I was a malignant overachiever, a hurried child. I missed my adolescence. I was middle-aged by the time I was twenty-one. So now we're even.

You know, it's funny. I had planned to invite several other recovering misery addicts whom I know fairly well to share their success stories in this chapter, but instead I've decided to tell mine. The AA model of story-telling that I will follow is based on Christ's interaction with the man He healed of mental illness.[1] The relieved man wanted to follow Jesus to the ends of the earth, but Jesus told him to go home and tell his peers what his earlier life had been like, what happened, and what his life was like after his healing.[2] I have decided to start this chapter (and end this trea-tise) by sharing briefly what it was like for me, what happened, and what it's like now.

Celebrating my imperfection

I am, and always have been, perfectly imperfect. How could I have been anything else? My youthful environment set me up to have unreal-istic expectations of myself and others. I was programmed to torture myself with merciless demands. I was my own worst enemy. But that's what created the pathology that drove me to recovery, so I'm thankful for it.

Step Five relieved me of the need to be perfect, and Step Ten allowed me to celebrate my humanity—to make mistakes and correct them by *promptly* admitting that I was wrong. I can honestly say that I'm com-fortable being human today. It's nice not to have to be as scrupulous as I once was. It's nice not to be constrained to defend my rightness and righteousness as fiercely as I once did. I can give myself and the people close to me a break, cut myself and them a whole lot of slack. Guess what? I'm having more fun, and I think they are too.

Accepting my humanity

The first three steps taught me that I'm not God and that I don't have to try to be all-seeing, all-knowing, all-wise. My faith and my relation-ship with my Higher Power are so much more relaxed than before.

I don't mean to discredit one of my favorite Bible characters, but I happen to think that the apostle Paul had an addictive personality (see Romans 7:15–24). He was totally engaged in being all things to all peo-ple and running races and fighting battles.[3] Good old Paul was my hero. Needless to say, I misused his example to justify a lot of my extreme, unhealthy behavior. That's not God's fault. I had an addictive and code-pendent mentality.

Self-acceptance—accepting myself as a fallible human being who doesn't have to try to be God—was one of the mini-spiritual awakenings that took place while I was en route to Step Twelve. A big part of my spiritual awakening was accepting and enjoying my humanity. Becoming totally OK with myself and dependent on a power greater than myself for my health and salvation has been, for me, both the journey and the destination.

So at the age of sixty-five, I'm right on schedule. I've told forty-five hundred clients in the last thirty-three years that *they* were right on schedule, but I wasn't sure that *I* was. I had to beat myself up once in awhile for being so retarded. Guess what? I *am* right on schedule. I'm entering the eighth stage of human development[4] and enjoying the outcome I had hoped for   genuine contentment and peace of mind.

There's another less desirable alternative for the outcome of this stage—one I was hoping to avoid. This other option is bitterness and remorse. Doesn't that sound like the misery and martyr syndrome? I sincerely believe that the Twelve Steps helped me get around that one and allowed me to experience the more positive outcome. At this point, I am looking forward to old age, which is about twenty years down the road.

Before I began my healing journey, I would have beaten myself up with self-criticism for taking so long to progress to the point where I am now. So what? It takes what it takes. I'm doing very well, thank you.

Occupying my life and relationships

Being fully present in my relationships has been a challenge for me because no one taught me how to do it. I've never been quite sure how to hang out with people. I know how to take care of them and fix them and rescue them and make them feel good about themselves. I know how to worry about them and wear myself out trying to "save" them. I know how to obsess about them and martyr myself over them. But I don't know how to hang out with them. In fact, I've always envied people who could. I have a couple of friends for whom casual as well as intimate relationships seem to come so naturally. With their help, I'm learning.

Occupying my soul and spirit

I'm satisfied that growing up in a dysfunctional environment left me undernurtured and overstressed. I was an immature, dispirited child in an adult body who grew up before her time. I was burned out emotionally on being an adult before I ever became one chronologically.

Being nurtured in twelve-step groups and practicing the steps as a way of life has helped me go back and pick up the stitches that were dropped. It has allowed me to grow myself up more gradually and gracefully than I otherwise might have. It's never too late to have a happy childhood!

I'm eternally grateful for the remedial program of character development called the Twelve Steps and for the *Big Book*–oriented Al-Anon sponsor God gave me—a sponsor who bases her program in AA literature. My best hope for every recovering misery addict is that they will find a sponsor and mentor like mine. Tina has been a wonderful spiritual guide throughout my journey.

I was sitting at a table in an Al-Anon meeting one morning, wondering why being there was such a blessing. Suddenly I realized that what was going on in that room was what healthy families do when they sit around the dinner table for a relaxed meal and enjoy each others' company. No fighting; no stone cold silences; no verbal violence; no icicles hanging from ten-foot poles; no sideways, passive-aggressive comments; no plates of spaghetti flying across the room; no controlling, caretaking, or advice giving; no guilt trips or shaming; no one being forced to eat food they don't like. Just a simple, sweet sharing. Just one family member asking another, "What's going on with you, and how do you feel about it?"

Mmmm, my Al-Anon meeting is like that—and it feels wonderful. It feels warm and healthy and caring and loving and safe. It makes me want to come back. This is known in twelve-step circles as the principle of attraction rather than promotion. Thank You, God. Please help me make my church more like that.

With the help of God and twelve-step fellowships, my spirit has been revived; the wounded child within me has grown and flourished. I am no longer depressed, discouraged, and dispirited. I am filled with wonder and gratitude. I enjoy greater self-awareness and a greater consciousness of God. Today, I can connect intimately with myself, with the God of my understanding, and with others. To me, that is the essence of spirituality.

Living in the moment

The experience of being right here, right now in this very moment, was foreign to me. I was dominated by the past, oriented to the future, and absent from today. I was always preoccupied. I was home, but the lights were out. Again, the experience of living the Twelve Steps has been the key to my being present in the moment.

Perhaps the most significant hallmark of where twelve-step programs have brought me is this: I'm writing this account—telling my story right now in "flow." This will be the first time in my life that I have written something and not criticized, edited, red-penciled, rewritten, rewritten, and rewritten it, worried about how it would be received and second-guessed every word. You're going to read it the way I wrote it the first time.

Celebrating myself

Jesus told fallible human beings like me to go and sin no more. Isn't that good news? This is what I hear in His words: "Little one, you don't have to make yourself miserable over past mistakes, over what other people think of you, over whether or not your loved ones act right, or over whether or not God is happy with you. He is. You're OK. Go and celebrate your humanity. Love yourself as much as I love you. Have fun. I'll be with you all the way."

Except ye become as little children—this is what recovery is all about. It's about regaining the purity and innocence that was ours in the beginning, recovering the me that was meant to be, discovering—or rediscovering—God as He really is, learning to love ourselves as we were first loved. Would you care to join me and several million others on the twelve-step journey to wholeness, happiness, and peace?

---

1. See Mark 5:1–18.
2. See Mark 5:19.
3. See 1 Corinthians 9:22–27.
4. See Appendix E.

Appendix A

Twenty Questions for Negaholics

1. When you wake up in the morning, are your first thoughts pessimistic?

2. If someone says, "Good morning," do you think, *What's good about it?*

3. Do you often feel inferior to others or "less than"?

4. Do you find it necessary to complain to friends, family, and even strangers about minor annoyances in your life?

5. When you walk into a room, do you immediately notice the negative—the flaws in the décor or the dust on the windowsill?

6. When you make new acquaintances, do you immediately notice their negative traits?

7. Do you open most conversations with a complaint?

8. Do you collect grievances against people and institutions?

9. When you talk about the traumas in your life, do you include more detail than necessary or exaggerate for effect?

10. Do you give more of your time, energy, or money to people and institutions than you can afford to give?

11. Do you fail to represent your rights in relationships because you don't want to hurt or offend others?

12. Do you hesitate to state your preferences to friends and family and then consider them inconsiderate if and when they don't meet your needs?

13. Do you accept unacceptable behavior, tolerate the intolerable?

14. Do you doubt people's sincerity?

15. Do you compare yourself unfavorably with others?

16. Do you invite people to take advantage of you?

17. Do you have an inordinate need for sympathy and attention?

18. Do you ever wish you could stop thinking so critically about yourself and others?

19. Have you tried your best to be more optimistic?

20. When you have failed, do you try harder?

Appendix B

**An Exhaustive (and Exhausting) List of Things
to Worry or Be Miserable About**

Before Arising

1. How tired I feel.
2. How to accomplish everything that needs to be done today.
3. Embarrassing things I said or did yesterday (last month, last year).
4. Maddening things other people said or did yesterday (last month, last year).
5. Problems that *may* arise today.
6. The future in general.
7. Anything whatsoever that I can possibly find to obsess about.
8. My love life (or lack thereof).

Upon Arising

1. My hair or my body.
2. My clothes.
3. My living circumstances.
4. My finances.
5. My diet or my health.
6. My job.
7. Getting my to-do list done.

8. My spouse's or children's behavior.
9. Stuff they haven't done yet but probably will.
10. My love life (or lack thereof).

Throughout the Day

1. What people think of me.
2. What people say about me.
3. The weather.
4. My parents, spouse, or kids.
5. Politics or current events.
6. My bills.
7. Making everybody happy.
8. Failing to make everybody happy.
9. Making the wrong decision.
10. Making the right decision.
11. Making any decision at all.
12. Making somebody angry or upset.
13. Hurting someone's feelings.
14. Boredom.
15. Fear of success or failure.
16. Fear of living or dying.
17. Flaws in myself and others.
18. My love life (or lack thereof).

At Bedtime

1. My love life (or lack thereof).
2. Loneliness.
3. Whether or not I will get a good night's sleep.
4. Whether or not I will have bad dreams.
5. How I will feel when I wake up.
6. How I will handle tomorrow's problems.
7. Whether or not I will be disapproved of, rejected by, or abandoned by anyone tomorrow.
8. Whether or not I'm a good enough Christian, parent, spouse, employee, etc.
9. Whether or not I matter.

10. Whether or not I will die before I wake.
11. Whether or not I will live before I die.
12. How I will be remembered when I die.
13. Whether or not I will be saved.
14. Whether or not God can actually handle things (such as my so briety, my salvation, or the sobriety and salvation of those I love).

Appendix C

A Little List of Martyring Behaviors
(Jeff Foxworthy style)

You might be a misery addict if . . .

you use negative terminology to describe neutral events.

you think of the future in terms of worst-case scenarios.

you get high from telling people how badly your boss, spouse, or children treat you.

you would rather complain than confront.

you whine instead of using your anger to energize yourself to take action.

you have your grudge list memorized.

you often walk away from conflict just before it is resolved.

you feel trapped and think you have no choices.

you believe that everything you try to do is doomed to failure.

you justify your misdeeds on the basis of other people's short comings.

you can't see your own defects of character for obsessing about someone else's.

you graciously invite people to take advantage of you and then resent it afterward.

you invite wolves (predators) into you life and then cry "wolf"
   (exploitation).

you exploit exploiters by using them to abuse you.

you use lack of time or money as a reason not to seek help when
   your life is falling apart.

you think it's selfish to take care of yourself.

There's a good chance you're a martyr if . . .

you're inclined to focus on what might have been.

you wear a pained expression on your face.

you use body language to communicate needs instead of asking
   for what you want.

you speak almost lovingly of your worries.

you discount compliments and disqualify people who try to affirm
   you.

you respond to insults with a "Thank you—that hurts so nice."

you find yourself humming the "Somebody Done Somebody
   Wrong Song" frequently.

your favorite spiritual is "All My Trials, Lord."

you're more animated when you describe being mistreated than
   at any other time.

you're at your best when you're managing a crisis.

you've turned grudge holding into a lifework.

you postpone calling the doctor when you're sick until it's time
   to call the undertaker.

you have trouble relaxing and having fun.

you can sacrifice yourself better than anybody else.

Appendix D

How to Distinguish Abstinence From Acting Out

"Using"
(taking the first drink)

1. Putting myself down.
2. Placing myself in a one-down position, (deferring to others).
3. Whining, complaining, acting helpless.
4. Mind reading, assuming insults.
5. Personalizing, internalizing people's remarks.
6. Manipulating to get attention instead of asking directly.
7. Isolating, not asking for what I need when feeling hurt or lonely.
8. Not asking for clarification when I take offense.

"Abstinence"
(putting the cork in the bottle)

1. Bypassing an opportunity to complain.
2. Refraining from obsessive analyzing.
3. Letting go and letting God, following good orderly direction.
4. Choosing a positive interpretation instead of a negative one (giving someone the benefit of the doubt when the odds are fifty-fifty).
5. Maintaining boundaries.
6. Asking directly for what I want and need in a timely way.
7. Not letting resentments build.

9. Remaining stuck in indecision because I don't want to make a mistake.
10. "Awfulizing."
11. Pouting.
12. Hurting myself, neglecting myself.
13. Shaming, second guessing myself.
14. Manifesting a hopeless attitude.
15. Giving up before I start, sabotaging my success.
16. Sympathy seeking.
17. Being overly apologetic.
18. Selling myself short.

8. Reality checking on a regular basis, especially when having a negative reaction.
9. Abstaining from criticism and second guessing.
10. Giving myself a pat on the back when I deserve it.
11. Accepting myself and passing God's unconditional approval along to my deepest self.
12. Being decisive, willing to risk making a mistake.
13. Not feeling guilty for feeling good.
14. Allowing myself to have fun.
15. Allowing myself to relax.
16. Being OK with who I *am,* instead of basing my self-esteem and value on what I *do.*

Appendix E

The Eight Stages of Human Development
(Erik Erickson)

Development Stage*	Age	Basic Lesson
1. Infancy	0–1 ½	Trust vs. mistrust
2. Early childhood	1½–3	Autonomy vs. shame, doubt
3. Preschool	3–5	Initiative vs. guilt
4. School age	5–12	Industry vs. inferiority
5. Adolescence	12–18	Identity vs. identity confusion
6. Young adulthood	18–24	Intimacy vs. isolation
7. Adulthood	24–65	Generative vs. stagnation
8. Senescence	65 +	Ego integrity vs. despair

* Stages are viewed as critical in the sense that each is built upon the successful completion of the previous stage.

NOTE: It is very likely that people who have been reared in dysfunctional environments as well as anyone who has experienced covert or overt trauma as a child is psychosocially stuck somewhere in the first four stages of development. Going back and doing the necessary developmental work is what recovery (therapy and twelve-step programs) is all about.

Appendix F

How to Handle Chronic Complainers

1. Don't ask negaholics how they're feeling.
2. Don't agree or disagree with their complaints.
3. Don't negate their feelings.
4. Don't try to reason with them or cheer them up.
5. Don't make suggestions or give advice.
6. Ask them if there is anything specific they would like you to do. This may help them focus.
7. Don't grab the ball and run with it.
8. Listen and empathize sincerely. Say something like, "That sounds terrible." "I don't know how you put up with all these problems." "I'm sorry this is happening." Then listen without further comment and excuse yourself as soon as possible.
9. If they accidentally say something positive, reinforce or reward that behavior. Let them know you enjoy being around them when they are positive and upbeat.
10. Don't complain about complainers to your other friends.

Appendix G

Twelve-Step Recovery Organizations

Adult Children of Alcoholics
P.O. Box 3216
Torrance, CA 90510
310-534-1815
www.adultchildren.org

Al-Anon/Alateen
1600 Corporate Landing Parkway
Virginia Beach, VA 23454-5617
757-563-1600
www.alanon.org

Alcoholics Anonymous
P.O. Box 459
New York, NY 10163
212-870-3400
www.aa.org

Cocaine Anonymous
3740 Overland Ave. Suite C
Los Angeles, CA 9003
310-559-5833
www.ca.org

Co-Dependents Anonymous (CoDA)
P.O. Box 33577
Phoenix, AZ 85067-3577
602-277-7991
www.coda.org

Codependents of Sex Addicts (CoSA)
P.O. Box 14537
Minneapolis, MN 55414
763-537-6904
www.cosa-recovery.org

Debtors Anonymous
P.O. Box 920888
Needham, MA 02492-0009
781-453-2743
www.debtorsanonymous.org

Incest Survivors Anonymous
P.O. Box 17245
Long Beach, CA 90807-7245
562-428-5599
www.lafn.org/medical/isa/home.html

Dual Recovery Anonymous
P.O. Box 8107
Prairie Village, KS 66208
877-883-2332
www.draonline.org

Marijuana Anonymous
P.O. Box 2912
Van Nuys, CA 91404
800-766-6779
www.marijuana-anonymous.org

Emotions Anonymous & E-Anon
P.O. Box 4245
St. Paul, MN 55104-0245
651-647-9712
www.emotionsanonymous.org

Nar-Anon
22527 Crenshaw Blvd., 200B
Torrance, CA 90505
800-477-6291
www.nar-anon.org

Families Anonymous
P.O. Box 3475
Culver City, CA 90231-3475
800-736-9805
www.familiesanonymous.org

Narcotics Anonymous
P.O. Box 9999
Van Nuys, CA 91409
818-773-9999
www.na.org

Gamblers Anonymous & Gam-Anon
P.O. Box 17173
Los Angeles, CA 90017
213-386-8789
www.gamblersanonymous.org

Nicotine Anonymous
419 Main St., PMB 370
Huntington Beach, CA 92648
415-750-0328
www.nicotine-anonymous.org

Obsessive Compulsive Anonymous
P.O. Box 215
New Hyde Park, NY 11040
516-739-0662
www.hometown.aol.com/west24th/

Sex & Love Addicts Anonymous
1550 NE Loop 410, Ste 118
San Antonio, TX 78209
210-828-7900
www.slaafws.org

Overeaters Anonymous
P.O. Box 44020
Rio Rancho, NM 87174-4020
505-891-2664
www.oa.org

Sexaholics Anonymous
P.O. Box 3565
Brentwood, TN 37024
866-424-8777
www.sa.org

Recovering Couples Anonymous
P.O. Box 11029
Oakland, CA 94611
510-663-2312
www.recovering-couples.org

Sexual Compulsives Anonymous
P.O. Box 1585
Old Chelsea Station
New York, NY 10011
800-977-4325
www.sca-recovery.org

S-Anon
P.O. Box 111242
Nashville, TN 37222-1242
615-833-3152
www.sanon.org

Survivors of Incest Anonymous
P.O. Box 190
Benson, MD 21018-9998
410-893-3322
www.siawso.org

Sex Addicts Anonymous
P.O. Box 70949
Houston, TX 77270
800-477-8191
www.sexaa.org

Workaholics Anonymous
World Service Organization
P.O. Box 289
Menlo Park, CA 94026-0289
510-273-9253
www.workaholics-anonymous.org

If you appreciated the message in this book, you'll want to read this one by the same author:

Never Good Enough

Carol Cannon

Did you grow up thinking you were never good enough? Do you still feel that way? It's time you learned to see yourself differently. The author uses actual case histories to explore the reasons behind addictive and codependent behaviors. In the pages of this eye-opening book you will learn that addiction is a no-fault disease and there is hope.

Paperback, 256 pages.
ISBN 13: 978-0-8163-1145-3
ISBN 10: 0-8163-1145-5

I Forgive You, But . . .

Lourdes E. Morales-Gudmundsson

This book is for Christians who believe that forgiveness is important to their spiritual journey but who may not understand what forgiveness really is. It's for those who just can't seem to move on from a deep hurt.

You find yourself mentioning the offense to a friend, remembering how the incident made you feel, and how it affected your life. Afterward, you feel guilty. Christians are to forgive and forget, right?

All could benefit from reading this intelligent and well-written explanation of forgiveness.

Paperback, 176 pages.
ISBN 13: 978-0-8163-2201-5
ISBN 10: 0-8163-2201-5.

Three ways to order:
1. Local Adventist Book Center®
2. Call 1-800-765-6955
3. Shop AdventistBookCenter.com